Practice*Planners*

Arthur E. Jongsma, Jr., Series Editor

Helping therapists help their clients...

Treatment Planners cover all the necessary elements for developing formal treatment plans, including detailed problem definitions, long-term goals, short-term objectives, therapeutic interventions, and DSM-IV™ diagnoses.

- ❑ The Complete Adult Psychotherapy Treatment Planner, Fourth Edition........978-0-471-76346-8 / $55.00
- ❑ The Child Psychotherapy Treatment Planner, Fourth Edition......................978-0-471-78535-4 / $55.00
- ❑ The Adolescent Psychotherapy Treatment Planner, Fourth Edition..............978-0-471-78539-2 / $55.00
- ❑ The Addiction Treatment Planner, Fourth Edition.....................................978-0-470-40551-2 / $55.00
- ❑ The Couples Psychotherapy Treatment Planner, Second Edition.................978-0-470-40695-3 / $55.00
- ❑ The Group Therapy Treatment Planner, Second Edition.............................978-0-471-66791-9 / $55.00
- ❑ The Family Therapy Treatment Planner, Second Edition............................978-0-470-44193-0 / $55.00
- ❑ The Older Adult Psychotherapy Treatment Planner ....978-0-471-29574-7 / $55.00
- ❑ The Employee Assistance (EAP) Treatment Planner ....978-0-471-24709-8 / $55.00
- ❑ The Gay and Lesbian Psychotherapy Treatment Planner ....978-0-471-35080-4 / $55.00
- ❑ The Crisis Counseling and Traumatic Events Treatment Planner ....978-0-471-39587-4 / $55.00
- ❑ The Social Work and Human Services Treatment Planner ....978-0-471-37741-2 / $55.00
- ❑ The Continuum of Care Treatment Planner..978-0-471-19568-9 / $55.00
- ❑ The Behavioral Medicine Treatment Planner...978-0-471-31923-8 / $55.00
- ❑ The Mental Retardation and Developmental Disability Treatment Planner ...978-0-471-38253-9 / $55.00
- ❑ The Special Education Treatment Planner..978-0-471-38872-2 / $55.00
- ❑ The Severe and Persistent Mental Illness Treatment Planner, Second Edition....978-0-470-18013-6 / $55.00
- ❑ The Personality Disorders Treatment Planner ....978-0-471-39403-7 / $55.00
- ❑ The Rehabilitation Psychology Treatment Planner ....978-0-471-35178-8 / $55.00
- ❑ The Pastoral Counseling Treatment Planner..978-0-471-25416-4 / $55.00
- ❑ The Juvenile Justice and Residential Care Treatment Planner ....978-0-471-43320-0 / $55.00
- ❑ The School Counseling and School Social Work Treatment Planner ....978-0-471-08496-9 / $55.00
- ❑ The Psychopharmacology Treatment Planner ....978-0-471-43322-4 / $55.00
- ❑ The Probation and Parole Treatment Planner...978-0-471-20244-8 / $55.00
- ❑ The Suicide and Homicide Risk Assessment & Prevention Treatment Planner ..978-0-471-46631-4 / $55.00
- ❑ The Speech-Language Pathology Treatment Planner...................................978-0-471-27504-6 / $55.00
- ❑ The College Student Counseling Treatment Planner ....978-0-471-46708-3 / $55.00
- ❑ The Parenting Skills Treatment Planner ....978-0-471-48183-6 / $55.00
- ❑ The Early Childhood Education Intervention Treatment Planner ....978-0-471-65962-4 / $55.00
- ❑ The Co-Occurring Disorders Treatment Planner...978-0-471-73081-1 / $55.00
- ❑ The Sexual Abuse Victim and Sexual Offender Treatment Planner ....978-0-471-21979-8 / $55.00
- ❑ The Complete Women's Psychotherapy Treatment Planner ....978-0-470-03983-0 / $55.00
- ❑ The Veterans and Active Duty Military Psychotherapy Treatment Planner ...978-0-470-44098-8 / $55.00

The **Complete Treatment and Homework Planners** series of books combines our bestselling *Treatment Planners* and *Homework Planners* into one easy-to-use, all-in-one resource for mental health professionals treating clients suffering from the most commonly diagnosed disorders.

- ❑ The Complete Depression Treatment and Homework Planner..................978-0-471-64515-3 / $48.95
- ❑ The Complete Anxiety Treatment and Homework Planner ....978-0-471-64548-1 / $48.95

Over 500,000 Practice*Planners*® sold ...

🟋 WILEY

Practice*Planners*®

Homework Planners feature dozens of behaviorally based, ready-to-use assignments that are designed for use between sessions, as well as a disk or CD-ROM (Microsoft Word) containing all of the assignments—allowing you to customize them to suit your unique client needs.

❏ Couples Therapy Homework Planner, Second Edition ....978-0-470-52266-0 / $55.00
❏ Child Psychotherapy Homework Planner, Second Edition ....978-0-471-78534-7 / $55.00
❏ Child Therapy Activity and Homework Planner...978-0-471-25684-7 / $55.00
❏ Adolescent Psychotherapy Homework Planner, Second Edition ....978-0-471-78537-8 / $55.00
❏ Addiction Treatment Homework Planner, Fourth Edition ....978-0-470-40274-0 / $55.00
❏ Employee Assistance Homework Planner ....978-0-471-38088-7 / $55.00
❏ Family Therapy Homework Planner, Second Edition ....978-0-470-50439-0 / $55.00
❏ Grief Counseling Homework Planner ....978-0-471-43318-7 / $55.00
❏ Divorce Counseling Homework Planner ....978-0-471-43319-4 / $55.00
❏ Group Therapy Homework Planner ....978-0-471-41822-1 / $55.00
❏ School Counseling and School Social Work Homework Planner................978-0-471-09114-1 / $55.00
❏ Adolescent Psychotherapy Homework Planner II.......................................978-0-471-27493-3 / $55.00
❏ Adult Psychotherapy Homework Planner, Second Edition.............................978-0-471-76343-7 / $55.00
❏ Parenting Skills Homework Planner ....978-0-471-48182-9 / $55.00

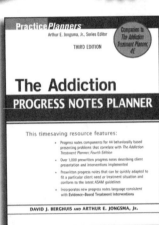

Progress Notes Planners contain complete prewritten progress notes for each presenting problem in the companion Treatment Planners.

❏ The Adult Psychotherapy Progress Notes Planner ....978-0-471-76344-4 / $55.00
❏ The Adolescent Psychotherapy Progress Notes Planner.............................978-0-471-78538-5 / $55.00
❏ The Severe and Persistent Mental Illness Progress Notes Planner ....978-0-470-18014-3 / $55.00
❏ The Child Psychotherapy Progress Notes Planner ....978-0-471-78536-1 / $55.00
❏ The Addiction Progress Notes Planner ....978-0-470-40276-4 / $55.00
❏ The Couples Psychotherapy Progress Notes Planner..................................978-0-471-27460-5 / $55.00
❏ The Family Therapy Progress Notes Planner..978-0-470-44884-7 / $55.00
❏ The Veterans and Active Duty Military
   Psychotherapy Progress Notes Planner..978-0-470-44097-1 / $55.00

Client Education Handout Planners contain elegantly designed handouts that can be printed out from the enclosed CD-ROM and provide information on a wide range of psychological and emotional disorders and life skills issues. Use as patient literature, handouts at presentations, and aids for promoting your mental health practice.

❏ Adult Client Education Handout Planner...978-0-471-20232-5 / $55.00
❏ Child and Adolescent Client Education Handout Planner ....978-0-471-20233-2 / $55.00
❏ Couples and Family Client Education Handout Planner...............................978-0-471-20234-9 / $55.00

Name _____

Affiliation _____

Address _____

City/State/Zip _____

Phone/Fax _____

E-mail _____

❏ Check enclosed   ❏ Visa   ❏ MasterCard   ❏ American Express

Card # _____

Expiration Date _____

Signature _____

Add $5 shipping for first book, $3 for each additional book. Please add your local sales tax to all orders. Prices subject to change without notice.

◼ **To order by phone in the US:**
   Call toll free 1-877-762-2974

◼ **Online: www.practiceplanners.wiley.com**

◼ **Mail this order form to:**
   John Wiley & Sons, Attn: J. Knott,
   111 River Street, Hoboken, NJ 07030

Couples Therapy
Homework Planner

Second Edition

Practice*Planners*® Series

Treatment Planners

The Complete Adult Psychotherapy Treatment Planner, Fourth Edition
The Child Psychotherapy Treatment Planner, Fourth Edition
The Adolescent Psychotherapy Treatment Planner, Fourth Edition
The Addiction Treatment Planner, Fourth Edition
The Continuum of Care Treatment Planner
The Couples Psychotherapy Treatment Planner, Second Edition
The Employee Assistance Treatment Planner
The Pastoral Counseling Treatment Planner
The Older Adult Psychotherapy Treatment Planner
The Behavioral Medicine Treatment Planner
The Group Therapy Treatment Planner, Second Edition
The Gay and Lesbian Psychotherapy Treatment Planner
The Family Therapy Treatment Planner, Second Edition
The Severe and Persistent Mental Illness Treatment Planner, Second Edition
The Mental Retardation and Developmental Disability Treatment Planner
The Social Work and Human Services Treatment Planner
The Crisis Counseling and Traumatic Events Treatment Planner
The Personality Disorders Treatment Planner
The Rehabilitation Psychology Treatment Planner
The Special Education Treatment Planner
The Juvenile Justice and Residential Care Treatment Planner
The School Counseling and School Social Work Treatment Planner
The Sexual Abuse Victim and Sexual Offender Treatment Planner
The Probation and Parole Treatment Planner
The Psychopharmacology Treatment Planner
The Speech-Language Pathology Treatment Planner
The Suicide and Homicide Risk Assessment & Prevention Treatment Planner
The College Student Counseling Treatment Planner
The Parenting Skills Treatment Planner
The Early Childhood Education Intervention Treatment Planner
The Co-Occurring Disorders Treatment Planner
The Complete Women's Psychotherapy Treatment Planner
The Veterans and Active Duty Military Psychotherapy Treatment Planner

Progress Notes Planners

The Child Psychotherapy Progress Notes Planner, Third Edition
The Adolescent Psychotherapy Progress Notes Planner, Third Edition
The Adult Psychotherapy Progress Notes Planner, Third Edition
The Addiction Progress Notes Planner, Third Edition
The Severe and Persistent Mental Illness Progress Notes Planner, Second Edition
The Couples Psychotherapy Progress Notes Planner
The Family Therapy Progress Notes Planner, Second Edition
The Veterans and Active Duty Military Psychotherapy Progress Notes Planner

Homework Planners

Brief Couples Therapy Homework Planner. Second Edition
Brief Family Therapy Homework Planner. Second Edition
Grief Counseling Homework Planner
Group Therapy Homework Planner
Divorce Counseling Homework Planner
School Counseling and School Social Work Homework Planner
Child Therapy Activity and Homework Planner
Addiction Treatment Homework Planner, Fourth Edition
Adolescent Psychotherapy Homework Planner II
Adolescent Psychotherapy Homework Planner, Second Edition
Adult Psychotherapy Homework Planner, Second Edition
Child Psychotherapy Homework Planner, Second Edition
Parenting Skills Homework Planner

Client Education Handout Planners

Adult Client Education Handout Planner
Child and Adolescent Client Education Handout Planner
Couples and Family Client Education Handout Planner

Complete Planners

The Complete Depression Treatment and Homework Planner
The Complete Anxiety Treatment and Homework Planner

Arthur E. Jongsma Jr., Series Editor

Couples Therapy Homework Planner

Second Edition

Gary M. Schultheis

Steffanie Alexander O'Hanlon

Bill O'Hanlon

WILEY

John Wiley & Sons, Inc.

Published by John Wiley & Sons, Inc., Hoboken, New Jersey.

Published simultaneously in Canada.

For general information on our other products and services please contact our Customer Care Department within the United States at (800) 762-2974, outside the United States at (317) 572-3993 or fax (317) 572-4002.

Wiley also publishes its books in a variety of electronic formats. Some content that appears in print may not be available in electronic books. For more information about Wiley products, visit our website at www.wiley.com.

Library of Congress Cataloging-in-Publication Data:
Schultheis, Gray M.
 Couples therapy homework planner / Gary M. Schultheis, Steffanie O'Hanlon, Bill O'Hanlon.—2nd ed.
     p. ; cm.—(PracticePlanners series)
 First published under title: Brief couples therapy homework planner, c2009.
 Includes bibliographical references.
  ISBN 978-0-470-52266-0 (pbk. : alk. paper); 978-0-470-64904-6 (ePDF); 978-0-470-64905-3 (eMobi);
  978-0-470-64906-0 (ePub).
  1. Marital psychotherapy—Problems, exercises, etc. 2. Brief psychotherapy—Problems exercises, etc. I. Schultheis, Gary M. II. O'Hanlon, Steffanie. III. O'Hanlon, William Hudson. Brief couples therapy homework planner. IV. Title. V Series: Practice planners.
  [DNLM: 1. Couples Therapy—Problems and Exercises. 2. Psychotherapy Brief—Problems and Exercises.
WM 18.2 S386b 2010]
RC488.5.S375 2010
616.89'456—dc22
                                                                          2010015497

Printed in the United States of America

10 9 8 7 6 5 4 3 2 1

CONTENTS

PRACTICE*PLANNERS*® SERIES PREFACE

Accountability is an important dimension of the practice of psychotherapy. Treatment programs, public agencies, clinics, and practitioners must justify and document their treatment plans to outside review entities in order to be reimbursed for services. The books and software in the Practice*Planners*® series are designed to help practitioners fulfill these documentation requirements efficiently and professionally.

The Practice*Planners*® series includes a wide array of treatment planning books, including not only the original *Complete Adult Psychotherapy Treatment Planner*, *Child Psychotherapy Treatment Planner*, and *Adolescent Psychotherapy Treatment Planner*, all now in their fourth editions, but also *Treatment Planners* targeted to specialty areas of practice, including:

- Addictions
- Behavioral medicine
- College students
- Co-occurring disorders
- Couples therapy
- Crisis counseling
- Early childhood education
- Employee assistance
- Family therapy
- Gays and lesbians
- Group therapy
- Juvenile justice and residential care
- Mental retardation and developmental disability
- Neuropsychology
- Older adults
- Parenting skills
- Pastoral counseling
- Personality disorders
- Probation and parole
- Psychopharmacology
- Rehabilitation psychology
- School counseling
- Severe and persistent mental illness
- Sexual abuse victims and offenders

- Social work and human services
- Special education
- Speech-language pathology
- Suicide and homicide risk assessment
- Women's issues

In addition, there are three branches of companion books that can be used in conjunction with the *Treatment Planners* or on their own:

- ***Progress Notes Planners*** provide a menu of progress statements that elaborate on the client's symptom presentation and the provider's therapeutic intervention. Each *Progress Notes Planner* statement is directly integrated with the behavioral definitions and therapeutic interventions from its companion *Treatment Planner*.

- ***Homework Planners*** include homework assignments designed around each presenting problem (such as anxiety, depression, chemical dependence, anger management, eating disorders, or panic disorder) that is the focus of a chapter in its corresponding *Treatment Planner*.

- ***Client Education Handout Planners*** provide brochures and handouts to help educate and inform clients on presenting problems and mental health issues, as well as life skills techniques. The handouts are included on CD-ROMs for easy printing from your computer and are ideal for use in waiting rooms, at presentations, as newsletters, or as information for clients struggling with mental illness issues. The topics covered by these handouts correspond to the presenting problems in the *Treatment Planners*.

The series also includes:

- **Thera***Scribe*®, the #1 selling treatment planning and clinical record-keeping software system for mental health professionals. Thera*Scribe*® allows the user to import the data from any of the *Treatment Planner*, *Progress Notes Planner*, or *Homework Planner* books into the software's expandable database to simply point and click to create a detailed, organized, individualized, and customized treatment plan along with optional integrated progress notes and homework assignments.

Adjunctive books, such as *The Psychotherapy Documentation Primer* and *The Clinical Documentation Sourcebook*, contain forms and resources to aid the clinician in mental health practice management.

The goal of our series is to provide practitioners with the resources they need in order to provide high-quality care in the era of accountability. To put it simply: We seek to help you spend more time on patients, and less time on paperwork.

ARTHUR E. JONGSMA, JR.
Grand Rapids, Michigan

ACKNOWLEDGMENTS

We want to thank our clients. They are collaborators in the work you find in these pages.

INTRODUCTION

Intimate relationships are the single most important predictor of life satisfaction. Yet in the United States, half of all first marriages and two-thirds of all second marriages end in divorce—daunting statistics. Since the first edition, entitled *Brief Couples Therapy Homework Planner,* was published in 1999, significant new research has been completed identifying attributes and skills that help couples thrive. This research has largely been undertaken by those in the emerging field of positive psychology. Brief solution-oriented therapy is one of the positive psychologies, which include other theoretical orientations as well (cognitive behavioral therapy [CBT], dialectical behavior therapy [DBT], mindfulness, narrative therapy, appreciative inquiry, etc.).

One of the most important factors identified in the research is the power of promoting the positive. Attributes such as commitment, good communication, accommodation, and vulnerability have been identified as factors enhancing relationship satisfaction and intimacy. In our culture we often set about problem solving with what is wrong and who is responsible in order to bring about change. This approach often results in an impasse, as it diminishes the very qualities associated with couple satisfaction. In the first and second editions of the *Couples Therapy Homework Planner,* homework assignments like "Catch Your Partner Doing Something Right" or "Little Things Mean a Lot" promote the expression of gratitude and positive regard. In the second edition, we have expanded the homework assignments to include material derived directly from our colleagues in the positive psychologies. There are several appreciative inquiry interviews, including "An Appreciative Interview to Celebrate the Anniversary of Your Marriage," as well as two assignments, "Breathing" and "Biodots," inspired by our mindfulness colleagues.

While we were pleased to find that the relationship attributes deemed most helpful were reflected in the first edition's homework assignments, we began to think that homework assignments are becoming more and more attractive to practitioners as a way to facilitate change, regardless of their therapeutic approach. Homework expands on work done in a session and allows clients to take what has been discussed in therapy and try it in the real world. We hope that this book will be helpful to those who are just learning to use homework assignments. In addition, this edition offers some new ideas to those who are experienced with homework but want to expand their use of this technique.

Brief therapy is especially appropriate for couples work. Most couples seek therapy only when their relationship is in serious trouble. If we don't offer help and activities to make some rapid changes, there is often no relationship left to work with.

We use homework assignments for many reasons, including that homework:

- Introduces change to the situation
- Encourages a spirit of experimentation
- Encourages clients to take an active part in therapy
- Evokes resources
- Highlights and allows follow-through on something that happened in the session
- Encourages the client to put more attention on an issue
- Encourages the client to take the next step before the next session
- Enhances the client's search for solutions

HOW TO USE THIS BOOK

This book is designed so that assignments can be easily copied from the disk and handed to clients. Many therapists work in situations where they don't have the luxury of time for creativity. This book will help fill the gaps caused by an overloaded schedule. While this is a legitimate way to use the book, we hope these assignments serve as a springboard for inspiration, encouraging therapists and clients to customize and create their own assignments. To make this process easier, we are providing a disk with forms that you can load on your computer and easily customize.

Years ago, we read an anecdote about the rock star Sting, who brought some songs he had just written to his two fellow band members. "Take these home and make them your own," he told them. When the band members were done, the song sounded better than when Sting had first written it. This is our model. Change things around and make the assignment your own. Delete questions you don't like. Work the couple's language and metaphors into the assignment. Rewrite the introductory paragraph. Invite your clients to help you. Don't forget to have fun (at least some of the time).

This is not a self-help book, a one-size-fits-all approach. These tasks are not appropriate for everyone. Use your judgment about whether an assignment is appropriate for any given situation. To assist you, these assignments are also cross-referenced with *The Couples Psychotherapy Treatment Planner* (O'Lears, Heyman, & Jongsma, 1998). Use your experience and personal expertise to guide you.

We have also included some introductory material detailing the model we chose to generate these homework assignments. More details and examples of the model can be found in some of our previous writings on relationships (Hudson & O'Hanlon, 1991; O'Hanlon & Hudson, 1995; O'Hanlon & O'Hanlon, 1998).

In addition, we have included some brochures that you can copy, personalize, and distribute to your clients. Feel free to modify these or generate your own. The more personalized you can make the handouts, the more participation you can expect from your clients.

ASSIGNING TASKS

It may be best to call these assignments tasks or experiments, not homework. That term evokes memories of meaningless activities handed out in school as busywork. Making the assignments relevant for clients is the way to ensure their cooperation. Task assignments are designed to bring about changes. We first make sure that we understand the problem that the client wants to change. By collaboratively designing tasks, we ensure that the assignments are relevant to the client. When the tasks are derived from a collaborative relationship, they are owned by both the practitioner and the client; that is, they are not "tasks" at all. Finally, we leave the client the option of discontinuing the assignment if the client feels that it is in his or her best interest to do so.

We have several ways to collaboratively design tasks. We offer clients multiple-choice possibilities and suggestions when presenting suggested actions. In addition, we provide clients with a preview of responses to similar assignments. During this process, we closely observe the clients' reactions. If a client shakes his or her head adamantly during such a preview or starts to shift uncomfortably, we consider that this might not be the best task for this particular client. Likewise, if a client is smiling or nodding or leaning forward, we know we are probably on the right track.

One therapist, Steffanie, saw a family that had been referred to her by their pediatrician because their 10-year-old son, Larry, had been having escalating temper tantrums since his surgery for severe colitis. The family had never been to therapy; however, they settled in quickly and readily discussed their son's colitis and temper tantrums. Steffanie reassured them about the likelihood of solving the problem and proceeded to tell them stories. She also provided examples of tasks that had worked for other families. The father began to shift in his chair and occasionally sigh as Steffanie spoke about these interventions. After observing this behavior, Steffanie turned to the father and said, "I think I'm off target in some way. I notice you seem uncomfortable when I start to talk about things to do." The father said, "You're telling us things *we* can do to stop the tantrums. We thought if we brought him here, *you* could work with him to stop the tantrums."

Steffanie and the family discussed psychotherapy. Steffanie presented her ideas and explained that she preferred to involve the family in making changes. After all, the family was really the expert on their son. She pointed out that they would be around when most of the tantrums occurred. Both parents seemed relieved, and the mother confided that they felt responsible for missing the warning signs of their son's illness and were scared to "do anything wrong again." They had come to mistrust their judgment and think "the professionals knew better." The family felt newly empowered to take control of the situation. They worked with Steffanie on developing new strategies for effectively dealing with tantrums.

DEBRIEFING

An essential part of using homework assignments is *debriefing* after the assignment has been carried out. Did the task make things better or worse? What did the client learn? Were there any problems? For us, this is the stuff of treatment. The feedback we receive from the assignment frequently creates the direction of the session. For instance, a therapist told a couple having fights regarding money about another couple he had worked with who had made a commitment to trying weekly budget "summits" at which they would make joint decisions about household expenditures. This couple agreed to do the task, but when they returned, they reported that it hadn't worked. In the ensuing discussion, the wife said, "He outtalks me every time and gets his way because he's better at arguing. He's like a lawyer and makes a forceful and persuasive case; I don't represent my side well." Knowing that, the therapist was able to help the couple hash out new ground rules for discussions that enabled them both to be heard and represented. This helped not only with the money discussions, but with other areas of difficulty they were having. Sometimes the brief therapy is criticized as "Band-Aid" therapy that doesn't deal with the real problem. On the contrary, we often find that when clients enhance their problem-solving skills during brief therapy, they can generalize those skills to other contexts.

We often tell our clients that the tasks are experiments. This has several advantages. One unspoken message is that we don't have the answers. Framing the exercise as an experiment implies that the therapist isn't expecting it to be the final truth about what will work. In this way, the therapist encourages and models flexibility and attention to results. When the client performs an exercise, either things improve or they don't. Either way, both clients and therapists get important information that can inform the next action to be taken. Sometimes clients ask why we have designed an assignment in a particular way. We answer them as honestly as possible.

Another way we have found to increase the likelihood of follow-through is to write the assignment down and follow up on it. We keep duplicate task forms so that we can give the client one copy and keep the other to refer to at the next session. Thus, clients have something concrete to refer to between sessions. It also makes us more likely to remember to follow up with clients the next session. Following up is very important: It communicates to the clients that the assignment wasn't just dreamed up to test their compliance.

When we first started to use homework assignments, we didn't get as much compliance as we do now. Because we were unsure if our clients would follow through, we sent them ambivalent messages about our expectations. Now we assume clients will do the tasks, and our language reflects this: "*After* you do this, I will want to follow up on how it went," rather than, "*If* you do this, let me know how it went." This simple step of presupposing the client will comply has made a dramatic difference. If clients do not do the assignment between sessions, we don't automatically assume they are being resistant. We discuss the assignment and ask what happened. Often we discover the assignment was not clear enough, it didn't fit, or clients have had a busy or overwhelming week.

When tasks are habitually not done, we use this analogy with clients: "I keep firing the starting pistol but you haven't left the blocks yet. You say you want to reach the finish line (your goal of fighting less, having more sex, doing better co-parenting, etc.), but you're still at the starting position looking at me as if to say, 'Why aren't we at the finish line yet?' The task we discussed is the starting pistol. Actions get you off the blocks and to the finish line."

When clients say they just don't have time or doing the task isn't a priority, we talk to them about whether they are motivated to work on the problem now and suggest they might want to return to therapy when they have the time and energy to focus on it. We have a general operating principle: The therapist should never be the most motivated person in the room. If you are more motivated than your clients, the whole therapy process will probably fail. Bill saw a sign in a restaurant once: "Never try to teach a pig to sing; it wastes your time and annoys the pig!" Perhaps you are trying to get people to do things that aren't right for them. You have an agenda for them that they are not motivated to fulfill. That is a no-win situation for you and your clients.

INTRODUCTION TO GENERIC TASKS

This section gives general interventions that can be helpful across many problem areas. The next section provides assignments for specific problem areas. Because this book is mostly about getting people to do things that change relationships, we want to make a brief note about the importance of listening and acknowledging in this approach. In brief couples therapy, our initial goal is to help each partner feel heard, understood, and validated without taking sides or deciding who is right or wrong. This is the validation part of therapy. Couples often enter therapy feeling blamed or discouraged. Our first task is to help them feel that their feelings and points of view, even if they are negative, are legitimate and understandable. At the same time, we have to be careful not to take sides or decide who is right while we are validating. And we must not communicate the idea that the situation is set in concrete. We want to, at the very least, create some sense that the situation is not hopeless. That means we quickly move into making changes. So, in addition to validating, we immediately set about helping the couple make changes in three areas around the problem:

1. What are they paying attention to in the problem situation, and how are they interpreting it? *(Changing the Viewing)*
2. How are they typically interacting with each other, including patterns of how each of them acts during the problem situation and how they talk with each other or others about the problem? We are searching for repeating patterns and helping couples change those problem patterns. *(Changing the Doing)*
3. What circumstances surround the problem? That is, what are the family backgrounds and patterns, the cultural backgrounds and patterns, the racial backgrounds, and the gender training and experiences that are contributing to the problem? In what locations do the couple's problems usually happen? *(Changing the Context)*

In each of these change areas, we have two tasks:

1. Recognizing and interrupting typical problem patterns
2. Seeking, highlighting, and encouraging solution patterns

When couples first enter therapy, they are typically focused on what is wrong and the problem parts of their situation. So we meet them there. But very early in the process of couples counseling, we also steer them toward telling us about times that have been better, moments when they solved the problems they were facing, incidents in which they were pleasantly surprised by their partner, or occasions when they found unexpected compassion or kindness during a stressful conflict. Most couples do not spontaneously report or even remember these "solution moments," but once prompted, they can recall and describe these solutions so that they become available for problem solving in the current situation. If a couple cannot identify solution moments, we might explore the ways that they have kept things from getting even worse than they are.

The following chart summarizes the three areas we focus our homework assignments on in couples therapy.

AREAS FOR INTERVENTION IN BRIEF COUPLES THERAPY

Viewing	Doing	Context
• Points of view • Attentional patterns • Interpretations • Explanations • Evaluations • Assumptions • Beliefs • Identity stories	• Action patterns • Interactional patterns • Language patterns • Nonverbal patterns	• Time patterns • Physical environmental/ spatial location • Cultural/racial background and propensities • Family/historical background and propensities • Biochemical/genetic background and propensities • Gender training and propensities • Connections to others • Spirituality
Challenge problem views that: *Blame* *Suggest that change is impossible* *Invalidate the person* *Suggest the person has no choice about his or her actions* Offer new possibilities for attention.	Find patterns that are part of the problem and that repeat. Suggest disrupting the problematic patterns or find and use solution patterns.	Suggest shifts in the context around the problem (e.g., changes in biochemistry, time, space, cultural habits, and influences). Use these areas to normalize (and therefore value and validate), as well as to find the problem and solution patterns in any or all of the contextual factors.

In brief couples therapy, we typically do not focus on historical issues or traumas that give rise to the couple's current difficulties. We focus more on the immediate problems that the couple is experiencing and help the parties make changes in those areas. The tasks that follow are congruent with this straightforward view of couples therapy but can be used with therapists of any theoretical orientation.

STACKING THE DECK

GOALS OF THE EXERCISE

1. To help clients identify their source of motivation.
2. To provide a personal reminder of desired results.

TYPES OF PROBLEMS THIS EXERCISE MAY BE MOST USEFUL FOR

- Any

SUGGESTIONS FOR PROCESSING THIS EXERCISE WITH THE COUPLE

1. Which card was most helpful overall?
2. What do you make of this?
3. Researchers studying happiness say relationships are more important than things in making us happy. Does your experience with this exercise support their findings?

STACKING THE DECK

Maintaining motivation can be a challenge. This exercise will help you keep your sense of purpose.

You will need a stack of three-by-five-inch cards. On each card you will put something you believe will help keep you on track to accomplish your goals. The more cards you make, the better. Keep them with you for times when you start to wander from the path, and review them at least once a day. Keep on the lookout for inspiration for more cards.

Here are some ideas for what you might include in your deck:

Quotations

Spiritual verses and prayers

Portraits

Vacation or other photos

Messages to yourself

Words of wisdom

Bumper stickers

Personal/inside jokes

Things that have worked

Things that might work

Drawings

Cartoons

You might want to keep a record of times you use your cards.

Date: _____   Time: _____

Describe the situation: _____

Which card was most helpful? _____

What changed? _____

Date: _____   Time: _____

    Describe the situation: _____

    Which card was most helpful? _____

    What changed? _____

Remember to bring completed worksheet to your next appointment.

PERSONAL PEP TALK

GOAL OF THE EXERCISE

1. To help clients clarify and maintain their motivation.

TYPES OF PROBLEMS THIS EXERCISE MAY BE MOST USEFUL FOR

*   Addictive Behaviors
*   Any Issue Where Sustained Effort Is Required

SUGGESTIONS FOR PROCESSING THIS EXERCISE WITH THE COUPLE

1. Tell me what you learned about what motivates you.
2. How did you use your video?
3. Was it helpful?
4. How might you make it more useful?

PERSONAL PEP TALK

Good intentions often get lost in time or obscured by emotion. This exercise can help you maintain your change-friendly state of mind.

For this exercise you need a digital camera capable of recording video or a computer with a camera and video recording software.

The task is to prepare a motivational pep talk for you to use in the future. Answer the following questions; then become your own coach and use your answers to create the text for your pep talk. Finally, create the video for your personal use.

1. What do you want for your relationship?

    _____

    _____

2. What is your motivation? Why is that important?

    _____

    _____

3. What are you willing to do to get what you want?

    _____

    _____

4. What do you need to keep in mind to reach your goal?

    _____

    _____

5. Add anything else that you think will help you.

    _____

    _____

Remember to bring completed worksheet to your next appointment.

GRAY AREAS

GOAL OF THE EXERCISE

1. To help clients resolve impasses and find common ground.

TYPES OF PROBLEMS THIS EXERCISE MAY BE MOST USEFUL FOR

*   Couples That Are Stuck and Polarized

SUGGESTIONS FOR PROCESSING THIS EXERCISE WITH THE COUPLE

1. Tell me what you learned about yourself and each other.
2. How was it helpful?
3. How might you make it more useful?

GRAY AREAS

*When partners are at an impasse, it can be helpful to explore gray areas in their think-
ing or exceptions to their positions. Negotiators use this technique to break down all-or-
nothing thinking and stereotypes, and to identify areas of possible midground. Couples,
like polarized nations, political antagonists, and labor disputants, make oversimplified
and inflexible assumptions about each other's points of view. Most of us are a bit more
complex and nuanced in our thinking and have a few exceptions, gray areas, or sometimes downright contradictions in our positions.*

Are there areas of exceptions in your point of view?

_____

_____

_____

Are there gray areas in your thinking? Gray areas are places where you may have
some doubts or are not fully convinced of your point of view.

_____

_____

_____

Create an argument justifying your partner's point of view or stance.

_____

_____

_____

Remember to bring completed worksheet to your next appointment.

LOVE-O-METER

GOALS OF THE EXERCISE

1. To encourage communication in couples who are very busy.
2. To provide a mode of communication to those who are not particularly good with words.
3. To increase awareness of problems.

TYPES OF PROBLEMS THIS EXERCISE MAY BE MOST USEFUL FOR

- Communications Issues
- Drifting Apart

SUGGESTIONS FOR PROCESSING THIS EXERCISE WITH THE COUPLE

1. What did you learn about what your partner wants?
2. How often did you check your partner's opinion?
3. Can you think of a way to share the same information that works better for you?

LOVE-O-METER

For any number of reasons, some couples find it difficult to let each other know how they feel about the relationship. You can get a simple read on the health of your relationship at any time with this exercise.

1. Obtain a deck of cards; each of you should choose a suit.

2. Choose a card, based on its value, that best represents your feelings about your satisfaction with the relationship.

3. Select a mutually agreeable place to leave both of your cards.

4. Review both cards at least once a day. You may change your card at any time to reflect your opinion.

    Note the events or behaviors that improved your opinion of the relationship.

    _____

    _____

    _____

    _____

    How did you respond to changes in your partner's card?

    _____

    _____

    _____

    Which of your own actions changed your opinion of the relationship?

    _____

    _____

    _____

Remember to bring completed worksheet to your next appointment.

SESSION PREPARATION

GOALS OF THE EXERCISE

1. To encourage clients to think about what they want to accomplish.
2. To encourage clients to take an active role in therapy.

TYPES OF PROBLEMS THIS EXERCISE MAY BE MOST USEFUL FOR

- All

SUGGESTION FOR PROCESSING THIS EXERCISE WITH THE COUPLE

1. Encourage clients to fax or e-mail you the completed form the day before the session.

SESSION PREPARATION

Name: _____ Date: _____

To get the most out of your next session, I suggest you take a few minutes to complete this form and fax or e-mail it to me the day before we meet.

What I have accomplished since our last session: my successes or victories:

- _____
- _____
- _____

What I didn't get done but want to be held accountable for:

- _____
- _____
- _____

Challenges I am facing right now:

- _____
- _____
- _____

What I am appreciative of or grateful/thankful for:

- _____
- _____
- _____

What I want to get out of the next session:

- _____
- _____
- _____

Remember to bring completed worksheet to your next appointment.

FEEDBACK LOG

GOALS OF THE EXERCISE

1. To encourage an attitude of experimentation.
2. To foster new behaviors.

TYPES OF PROBLEMS THIS EXERCISE MAY BE MOST USEFUL FOR

- Anger Management
- Communication Issues

SUGGESTIONS FOR PROCESSING THIS EXERCISE WITH THE COUPLE

1. When you managed to control your temper, how was your thinking different?
2. What might you do to help you remember what you've learned?

FEEDBACK LOG

Things are not always going to go the way we want. Why does that upset us? You may be able to change the way you think so that everyday challenges don't get under your skin so often. Expectations are usually at the heart of this irritation. When things don't go your way, learn to see it as a lesson on what works and what doesn't rather than as a failure. If you can adopt this new way of thinking, you will get smarter every day.

Find one event each day that irritated or frustrated you, and answer the following questions:

Date: _____

What happened?

_____

_____

What was your first reaction? What went through your head?

_____

_____

What can you learn about yourself, others, and the world from this experience?

_____

_____

_____

_____

_____

Date: _____

What happened?

_____

_____

What was your first reaction? What went through your head?

_____

_____

What can you learn about yourself, others, and the world from this experience?

_____

_____

_____

_____

_____

Date: _____

What happened?

_____

_____

What was your first reaction? What went through your head?

_____

_____

What can you learn about yourself, others, and the world from this experience?

_____

_____

_____

_____

_____

Date: _____

What happened?

_____

_____

What was your first reaction? What went through your head?

_____

_____

What can you learn about yourself, others, and the world from this experience?

_____

_____

_____

_____

_____

Date: _____

What happened?

_____

_____

What was your first reaction? What went through your head?

_____

_____

What can you learn about yourself, others, and the world from this experience?

_____

_____

_____

_____

_____

Date: _____

What happened?

_____

_____

What was your first reaction? What went through your head?

_____

_____

What can you learn about yourself, others, and the world from this experience?

_____

_____

_____

_____

_____

Remember to bring completed worksheet to your next appointment.

LEARNING THE LANGUAGE

GOALS OF THE EXERCISE

1. To encourage participants to talk about what they need.
2. To make communication more effective.

TYPES OF PROBLEMS THIS EXERCISE MAY BE MOST USEFUL FOR

*   Boredom
*   Estrangement

SUGGESTIONS FOR PROCESSING THIS EXERCISE WITH THE COUPLE

1. How did you use the information you received from your partner?
2. What did you do when you didn't get the response you wanted?

LEARNING THE LANGUAGE

Rate these activities for their ability to communicate love and caring to you from your spouse. Feel free to edit them or add to the list.

Plan an evening out.

Say "I love you" with those or other words.

Initiate sex.

Fix the thing I asked you to.

Be nice to my mother.

Tell me about your day.

Listen, really listen, as I tell you about my day.

Tell me a secret.

Tell me your dreams.

Give me an afternoon by myself to do what I want.

Show affection without expecting sex.

Lower the toilet seat.

Prepare my favorite meal.

Surprise me with a small gift.

Throw me a surprise party.

Wash my car.

Go to church with me.

Play with the kids.

Give the baby a bath and put her to bed.

Pick up your stuff.

Do the grocery shopping.

Laugh at my jokes.

Remember to bring completed worksheet to your next appointment.

CHART YOUR COURSE

GOALS OF THE EXERCISE

1. To encourage the couple to clarify what they want.
2. To suggest that the couple focus on the goal of therapy rather than focusing so much on the problem.

TYPES OF PROBLEMS THIS EXERCISE MAY BE MOST USEFUL FOR

- Disillusionment with Relationship
- Infidelity
- Jealousy
- Life-Changing Events
- Loss of Love/Affection
- Midlife Crisis
- Personality Differences
- Separation and Divorce

SUGGESTIONS FOR PROCESSING THIS EXERCISE WITH THE COUPLE

1. How will you know therapy has been successful?
2. What will be or what has been the first sign of change?
3. What will you do to encourage change to continue?

CHART YOUR COURSE

Aimless wandering can be an enjoyable and sometimes profitable activity; however, if you want to accomplish something, you'll probably find that it's best not to count on serendipity to save the day. Pilots are required to file a flight plan before taking off. Lenders require a business plan before they lend money. If you haven't defined goals for your relationship recently, you may find this exercise helpful in getting you started making the changes you are looking for.

Between now and your next session, make a list of the things you would like to change in your relationship.

_____
_____
_____
_____
_____
_____
_____
_____
_____
_____

Which of these are under your control?

_____
_____
_____
_____
_____

When you are finished with counseling, what will be different that will make you able to look back on the things you wanted to change and say to yourself, "Getting into counseling and doing the work I did there was one of the best things I've ever done for myself and my relationship"?

_____

_____

_____

_____

_____

_____

What will be or perhaps has been the first and smallest sign that change is beginning?

_____

_____

_____

_____

_____

When you notice that first change, what will you do to keep the ball rolling?

_____

_____

_____

_____

_____

_____

How will these changes improve your life? Why are they significant?

_____

_____

_____

_____

_____

_____

Remember to bring completed worksheet to your next appointment.

TAKING CHARGE OF CHANGE

GOALS OF THE EXERCISE

1. To get each partner to start taking responsibility for making changes rather than waiting for the other person to change.
2. To communicate the idea that one person can change a relationship.

TYPES OF PROBLEMS THIS EXERCISE MAY BE MOST USEFUL FOR

- Communication
- Dependency
- Disillusionment with Relationship
- Infidelity
- Life-Changing Events
- Loss of Love/Affection
- Midlife Crisis
- Personality Differences
- Separation and Divorce
- Work/Home Role Strain

SUGGESTIONS FOR PROCESSING THIS EXERCISE WITH THE COUPLE

1. What were the things you noticed that you could have done differently?
2. Did you do anything differently as a result of completing this exercise?
3. What changed as a result of your completing this exercise?

TAKING CHARGE OF CHANGE

Even if the other person is, in your view, the source of the problem, there are things you can do to take back your power and to make a difference in the relationship. This exercise may help you find the places where you have some personal power.

Describe three situations that occur between now and your next session that are representative of something you would like to change in your relationship. In your description, focus on what you do or experience in the situation, rather than how you want the other person to change. Pay special attention to things that you may say or do, rather than what your partner does. Note how you respond to your partner. Write your description as objectively as possible, as if you are an uninvolved third party. After you write your description, let it rest for a day. Then study it and look for as many things as possible that you might have done differently that would have changed the event. Be ready to discuss these ideas with your therapist in your next session.

Situation 1

What happened?

_____

_____

_____

_____

What could you have done differently?

_____

_____

_____

_____

Situation 2

What happened?

_____
_____
_____
_____

What could you have done differently?

_____
_____
_____
_____

Situation 3

What happened?

_____
_____
_____
_____

What could you have done differently?

_____
_____
_____
_____

Situation 4

What happened?

_____
_____
_____
_____

What could you be done differently?

_____
_____
_____
_____

Remember to bring completed worksheet to your next appointment.

UNPACK LOADED AND VAGUE WORDS

GOALS OF THE EXERCISE

1. To help move couples from vague or blaming communications to more specific and change-oriented talk.
2. To help you, the therapist, get a better picture of what is happening with the couple.

TYPES OF PROBLEMS THIS EXERCISE MAY BE MOST USEFUL FOR

- Anger
- Anxiety
- Blame
- Communication
- Dependency
- Intolerance
- Jealousy

SUGGESTIONS FOR PROCESSING THIS EXERCISE WITH THE COUPLE

1. How was this exercise helpful to you?
2. What did you learn by doing this exercise that surprised you?
3. How did it feel different using "videotalk" rather than your usual way of talking?

UNPACK LOADED AND VAGUE WORDS

Have you noticed that when you use certain words or phrases you can get a rise out of your partner? For example, you might find that when you say things like "You're being selfish" or "You're just like your father," your partner reacts badly. You might think of these words as packaged words—words and phrases that may mean something specific to you, but that have meanings that are not clear to your partner. It's often best to unpack those vague words and phrases and get specific. The simplest way to defuse such phrases and words is to translate them into action descriptions or what could be called "videotalk": Use words that describe what you could see and hear on a videotape, rather than using more vague or judgmental words. So, instead of saying, "Well, when you were judging me, I got defensive," you could try saying, "When you pointed your finger at me and said I was immature, I got defensive." Instead of telling your partner that the problem is what he or she is, it is usually less threatening and more conducive to change to focus on what he or she does that is a problem for you. This exercise is designed to help you unpack your vague or provocatively labeled word box.

1. Think of three things that your partner does or has done recently that you don't like, and list them here as you would normally express them.

    _____
    _____
    _____
    _____

2. Translate each complaint into videotalk.

    _____
    _____
    _____
    _____

3. Find an appropriate time and, using videotalk, tell your partner the three things that he or she has done that you haven't liked. Do not give your ideas about why your partner did it or a prediction about what he or she will do about it in the future. Avoid generalizing or labeling. Get specific about what it looked like and sounded like in one particular instance.

_____

_____

_____

_____

4. Invite your partner to tell you three things that you have done that he or she hasn't liked.

_____

_____

_____

_____

5. If your partner gives you a theory or story or is vague, gently steer him or her back to getting specific with videotalk by suggesting that you really want to know what he or she would like you to change.

_____

_____

_____

_____

6. Write your partner's complaints in videotalk.

_____

_____

_____

_____

7. How did videotalk change your interaction?

_____

_____

_____

_____

8. What, if anything, was difficult for you about using videotalk?

    _____
    _____
    _____
    _____

9. Do you have any objection to using videotalk in the future?

    _____
    _____
    _____
    _____

Remember to bring completed worksheet to your next appointment.

DOING LOVE AND INTIMACY

GOALS OF THE EXERCISE

1. To get couples to begin to act in more kind and loving ways to one another.
2. To communicate the idea that feelings can change and be affected by actions.

TYPES OF PROBLEMS THIS EXERCISE MAY BE MOST USEFUL FOR

*   Anger
*   Communication
*   Disillusionment with Relationship
*   Infidelity
*   Intolerance
*   Jealousy
*   Loss of Love/Affection
*   Midlife Crisis
*   Personality Difference
*   Separation and Divorce
*   Sexual Dysfunction

SUGGESTIONS FOR PROCESSING THIS EXERCISE WITH THE COUPLE

1. Did you feel more loving as you did more loving things?
2. Did your partner seem more loving to you?
3. How could you use what you learned from doing this exercise in the future in your relationship?

DOING LOVE AND INTIMACY

Sometimes people are waiting for the feelings they used to have to come back. Another approach that sometimes works better is to take action even if you don't feel like it to see what feelings arise. If you are not feeling love or intimacy right now, examine how lovingly and intimately you are behaving. Try acting loving for a period of time and find out if you start to feel more love. In choosing your actions, think back on what has worked in the past and what your partner has asked for.

1. Write in detail five things you could do to express love for your partner. For the purpose of this exercise, make it five things that do not depend on the active participation of your partner.

    _____

    _____

    _____

    _____

    _____

2. For the next two weeks, do any of those five things each day with your partner. If you get ideas for more than five things, feel free to add those things to your repertoire of behaviors. Record your experience here for each day.

Day 1

What did you do?

_____

_____

What did you learn?

_____

_____

Day 2

What did you do?

_____

_____

What did you learn?

_____

_____

Day 3

What did you do?

_____

_____

What did you learn?

_____

_____

Day 4

What did you do?

_____

_____

What did you learn?

_____

_____

Day 5

What did you do?

_____

_____

What did you learn?

_____

_____

Day 6

What did you do?

_____

_____

What did you learn?

_____

_____

Day 7

What did you do?

_____

_____

What did you learn?

_____

_____

Day 8

What did you do?

_____

_____

What did you learn?

_____

_____

Day 9

What did you do?

_____

_____

What did you learn?

_____

_____

Day 10

What did you do?

_____

_____

What did you learn?

_____

_____

Day 11

What did you do?

_____

_____

What did you learn?

_____

_____

Day 12

What did you do?

_____

_____

What did you learn?

_____

_____

Day 13

What did you do?

_____

_____

What did you learn?

_____

_____

Day 14

What did you do?

_____

_____

What did you learn?

_____

_____

Remember to bring completed worksheet to your next appointment.

TRACK THE PROBLEMS AND SOLUTIONS

GOALS OF THE EXERCISE

1. To get a reading on the severity of the couple's problems.
2. To communicate the awareness that problems are not constant and can change in intensity, severity, and frequency.

TYPES OF PROBLEMS THIS EXERCISE MAY BE MOST USEFUL FOR

- Anger
- Anxiety
- Blame
- Communication
- Depression
- Eating Disorder
- Financial Conflict
- Job Stress
- Parenting Conflicts

SUGGESTIONS FOR PROCESSING THIS EXERCISE WITH THE COUPLE

1. What did you learn about what made the problem better or worse?
2. What could you do in the future with what you learned from this exercise to improve your relationship?

TRACK THE PROBLEMS AND SOLUTIONS

Every day brings the opportunity to learn from experience. If you pay attention only to your failures or problems, you may learn what not to do, but you miss many chances to go further in the directions that have been helpful. This is an exercise to help you become more aware of your success so you can put it to good use.

Choose a time each day to think about your situation. At that time, create an imaginary scale from 0 to 10 that ranges from the worst your situation could possibly be to absolute utopia (don't forget that *utopia* is translated literally as "not place"). Now place yourself on that scale and check the box next to the appropriate number. Note anything that you have done that has helped you or your relationship. If you are feeling down today, note what you have done that kept things from getting even worse. If two of you are doing this exercise, realize that your partner will be likely to have a different way of looking at the situation and there is no reason why your experiences have to match. Note elsewhere how the two of you handle differences in your experiences. Use another sheet of paper if necessary.

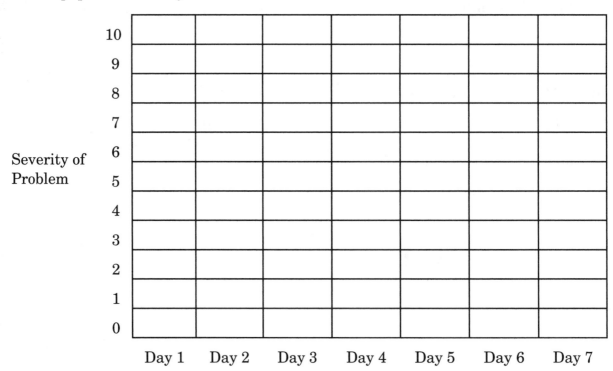

Remember to bring completed worksheet to your next appointment.

IDENTIFY AND VALIDATE YOUR PARTNER'S FEELINGS AND POINTS OF VIEW

GOALS OF THE EXERCISE

1. To help the couple listen to and stop blaming one another.
2. To clarify miscommunications and misunderstandings.

TYPES OF PROBLEMS THIS EXERCISE MAY BE MOST USEFUL FOR

- Communication
- Financial Conflict
- Jealousy
- Job Stress
- Life-Changing Events
- Midlife Crisis
- Parenting Conflict
- Religion/Spirituality Differences
- Values Conflicts
- Work/Home Role Strain

SUGGESTIONS FOR PROCESSING THIS EXERCISE WITH THE COUPLE

1. How did it feel for you to be listened to and validated?
2. How did it feel to listen and validate?
3. What surprised you in doing this exercise?

IDENTIFY AND VALIDATE YOUR PARTNER'S FEELINGS AND POINTS OF VIEW

Sometimes the simplest solution is to just stop and listen to what your partner is saying and imagine how he or she could be feeling that way or seeing things in that light.

Try this experiment between now and your next session. Choose three situations when your partner is complaining about you or something you did. Don't try to defend yourself, correct your partner's perceptions, or talk him or her out of those feelings. Just put yourself in your partner's position and try to hear how he or she understands, interprets, and feels about the situation. Imagine how you would feel or act if you were seeing things that way. (If what your partner is saying sounds crazy or unreasonable, consider the possibility that you are missing something, and listen and ask questions to see if you can understand.) Express that understanding and let your partner know how difficult it must be, given how he or she is feeling about the situation.

Record your experiences for each situation:

1. What was your partner's complaint?

    _____

    _____

    _____

    _____

    _____

    _____

2. What did you learn by listening?

    _____

    _____

    _____

    _____

    _____

    _____

    _____

3. How did changing your behavior affect the interaction?

    _____

    _____

    _____

    _____

    _____

    _____

Remember to bring completed worksheet to your next appointment.

CHANGING CHARACTER INDICTMENTS TO ACTION DESCRIPTIONS

GOALS OF THE EXERCISE

1. To help couples change their unproductive criticism and conflict patterns.
2. To help couples get specific in their complaints in order to make the possibility of change more likely.

TYPES OF PROBLEMS THIS EXERCISE MAY BE MOST USEFUL FOR

- Blended-Family Problems
- Communication
- Financial Conflict
- Jealousy
- Job Stress
- Life-Changing Events
- Midlife Crisis
- Religion/Spirituality Differences
- Work/Home Role Strain

SUGGESTIONS FOR PROCESSING THIS EXERCISE WITH THE COUPLE

1. How did this descriptive process feel different to you?
2. Did you get any new ideas about your partner from doing this exercise?
3. Did you notice anything that improved as a result of doing this exercise?

CHANGING CHARACTER INDICTMENTS TO ACTION DESCRIPTIONS

It's very difficult to build bridges at the same time that you are building walls. If you attack another person verbally, you can expect that individual to put up a defense, which can make communication difficult. When you want to talk about something someone did that upset you, try talking about the behavior rather than about the person's character or something else that is very difficult for the individual to change.

Each time you find yourself in a situation where you would customarily lash out about your partner's flaws, rather than proceed as usual, substitute a description of the behavior you object to. Stick to a factual description of what happened, and explain clearly what you would like your partner to do instead.

Record the incident. Then write a clear description of exactly what happened. Stick to things that you can see and hear in your description.

Date: _____ Time: _____

Place: _____

Describe the behavior that you objected to:

_____

_____

_____

_____

_____

_____

_____

What did you say?

_____

_____

_____

What difference do you think that your change in language made?

_____

_____

_____

Date: _____ Time: _____

Place: _____

Describe the behavior that you objected to:

_____

_____

_____

What did you say?

_____

_____

_____

What difference do you think that your change in language made?

_____

_____

_____

Remember to bring completed worksheet to your next appointment.

IDENTIFY WHAT HAS WORKED AND DO MORE OF THAT

GOALS OF THE EXERCISE

1. To invite couples to look at a problem in more detail with an eye toward finding solutions.
2. To further suggest that each partner may be able to affect the problem.

TYPES OF PROBLEMS THIS EXERCISE MAY BE MOST USEFUL FOR

- Anger
- Blame
- Communication
- Dependency
- Life-Changing Events
- Parenting Conflicts
- Recreational Activities Disputes
- Sexual Dysfunction
- Work/Home Role Strain

SUGGESTIONS FOR PROCESSING THIS EXERCISE WITH THE COUPLE

1. When was the problem less serious?
2. What did you do to influence the problem?
3. What did you learn from this exercise?

IDENTIFY WHAT HAS WORKED AND DO MORE OF THAT

One way to solve problems is to look at what you are already doing that works and do it more. The difficulty is that unless you are looking for the successes, especially the small ones, they can go unnoticed. Chances are that you know more than you think you do.

Identify 10 things that you and your partner do well. For each of the 10 things, identify three skills that are used in that behavior. For example:

Ex. We make time for ourselves.

    Skills: We both make this a priority.

            We share our schedules and plans.

            We take turns choosing our activities.

1. _____

    Skills: _____

        _____

        _____

2. _____

    Skills: _____

        _____

        _____

3. _____

    Skills: _____

        _____

        _____

4. _____

    Skills: _____

        _____

        _____

5. _____

Skills: _____

_____

_____

6. _____

Skills: _____

_____

_____

7. _____

Skills: _____

_____

_____

8. _____

Skills: _____

_____

_____

9. _____

Skills: _____

_____

_____

10. _____

Skills: _____

_____

_____

Consider the skills that you demonstrate and identify any that might help you in situations where you have been having difficulty.

Remember to bring completed worksheet to your next appointment.

LITTLE THINGS MEAN A LOT

GOALS OF THE EXERCISE

1. To get the couple to notice that there are aspects of their relationship that are fine.
2. To reorient the couple's attention to the parts of their relationship that are working rather than those that are problematic.

TYPES OF PROBLEMS THIS EXERCISE MAY BE MOST USEFUL FOR

- Anger
- Anxiety
- Blended-Family Problems
- Depression
- Disillusionment with Relationship
- Loss of Love/Affection
- Religion/Spirituality Differences
- Separation and Divorce
- Sexual Dysfunction

SUGGESTIONS FOR PROCESSING THIS EXERCISE WITH THE COUPLE

1. Were you surprised that there were some aspects of your relationship that you didn't want to change or that were working fine?
2. How did focusing on those aspects change your view of or feelings about the relationship?
3. Did you get any ideas for things you might be able to do to change your relationship for the better through doing this exercise?

LITTLE THINGS MEAN A LOT

Each day note here three things regarding the relationship that you do NOT want to change. Notice times when you and your partner handle a situation well or at least better than you had expected. Note your part in making these things happen or continue to happen.

Day 1

1. _____
2. _____
3. _____

Day 2

1. _____
2. _____
3. _____

Day 3

1. _____
2. _____
3. _____

Day 4

1. _____
2. _____
3. _____

Day 5

1. _____
2. _____
3. _____

Day 6

1. _____
2. _____
3. _____

Day 7

1. _____
2. _____
3. _____

Day 8

1. _____
2. _____
3. _____

Day 9

1. _____
2. _____
3. _____

Day 10

1. _____
2. _____
3. _____

Remember to bring completed worksheet to your next appointment.

KEEP ONE EYE ON THE ROAD

GOALS OF THE EXERCISE

1. To get couples oriented to how to change rather than how they are stuck.
2. To get couples to notice and acknowledge small signs of progress rather than having to see big changes to feel hopeful or better about the relationship.

TYPES OF PROBLEMS THIS EXERCISE MAY BE MOST USEFUL FOR

*   Alcohol Abuse
*   Blame
*   Dependency
*   Depression
*   Eating Disorder
*   Physical Abuse
*   Psychological Abuse
*   Sexual Abuse

SUGGESTIONS FOR PROCESSING THIS EXERCISE WITH THE COUPLE

1. Was thinking about what you wanted to have happen and noticing any small steps toward that helpful?
2. Was thinking about what you want more helpful than thinking about all the things you don't want or haven't liked?
3. What little signs did you notice that were good signs?

KEEP ONE EYE ON THE ROAD

A story is told of an unfortunate vacationer taking photos at the Grand Canyon who was so focused on the image in the viewfinder that he failed to notice the canyon's edge. While less dramatic, there are dangers in failing to see what's right in front of you in everyday life. If you want changes in your relationship and you fail to see and acknowledge small successes or improvements, you run the risk of squelching change before it gets a good start. This exercise will help you learn to watch for those little signs of improvement that can become monumental.

1. Describe what you want to happen.

    _____

    _____

2. Write at least five things that would represent movement toward your goal.

    _____

    _____

    _____

    _____

    _____

3. Between now and your next session, note anything that happens that you see as a step in the right direction and be ready to discuss how it came about.

    _____

    _____

    _____

    _____

Remember to bring completed worksheet to your next appointment.

TIME TRAVEL

GOALS OF THE EXERCISE

1. To get the couple thinking in terms of solutions rather than in terms of problems.
2. To get the couple focused more on the present and the future than on the past.

TYPES OF PROBLEMS THIS EXERCISE MAY BE MOST USEFUL FOR

- Anger
- Blame
- Communication
- Dependency
- Infidelity
- Life-Changing Events
- Midlife Crisis

SUGGESTIONS FOR PROCESSING THIS EXERCISE WITH THE COUPLE

1. What were your five actions that would lead to that preferred future?
2. What three changes in thinking would you make if that were your future?
3. What did you learn from doing this exercise?

TIME TRAVEL

This exercise involves imagining that a problem is solved and describing what is different in that future. It is a bit like riding in a backward-facing seat in a train. You get an entirely different view than if you are facing forward. Strangely, the shift in perspective can get your mind off the problems and on solutions. Then you can work backwards from the solution future to the present with this new mindset.

1. Imagine that the relationship problem or problems you've been struggling with are resolved. Things worked out well for both of you. Nobody lost. This might take some imagination, but do your best. After you've imagined yourself in that place for a while, write a detailed description of your life and your relationship where the problem is solved.

   _____

   _____

   _____

   _____

   _____

   _____

2. Write five things that you would do or say differently right now if you knew for certain that you were headed toward that future.

   _____

   _____

   _____

   _____

3. List three things you would think about differently if you knew for an absolute fact that you were headed toward that future.

   _____

   _____

   _____

4. What effect would it have if you started doing those things even though the outcome is uncertain?

_____

_____

_____

_____

5. What adjustments will you have to make or things will you have to start doing knowing that there are no guarantees of success?

_____

_____

_____

_____

Remember to bring completed worksheet to your next appointment.

WHAT IS YOUR MAP OF LOVE-LAND?

GOALS OF THE EXERCISE

1. To get couples to realize that they often have different definitions and criteria for love and affection.
2. To help couples teach one another about those differences.

TYPES OF PROBLEMS THIS EXERCISE MAY BE MOST USEFUL FOR

- Communication
- Dependency
- Disillusionment with Relationship
- Infidelity
- Jealousy
- Loss of Love/Affection
- Personality Differences

SUGGESTIONS FOR PROCESSING THIS EXERCISE WITH THE COUPLE

1. What surprised you about what your partner said or wrote?
2. What did you learn about yourself from doing this?
3. How will doing this exercise change your relationship?

WHAT IS YOUR MAP OF LOVE-LAND?

We each have our own ideas, our own map of love-land. They often come about based on various family, personal, and cultural experiences and expectations. One partner's candy-cane forest may be the other partner's molasses swamp. Trouble comes in couples relationships when we assume/expect our partner's map to be the same as ours. This exercise helps each member of the couple survey and outline his or her own map of love-land. With maps in hand, each person can then communicate their expectations so that in the future they will both be aware of what the other person is looking for. One caution is that all maps change over time, so plan to make revisions. An outdated map can be as bad as no map at all.

Give three examples of your idea of a romantic evening.

_____

_____

_____

What is your ideal balance of time alone versus couples time?

_____

_____

_____

_____

What are three things you like to do together that cost no money?

_____

_____

_____

When have you felt most loved in the past three years?

_____

_____

_____

_____

When have you felt closest in your relationship?

_____

_____

_____

_____

When have you felt most valued in the past three years?

_____

_____

_____

_____

What are five things your partner does to communicate that he or she cares about you?

_____

_____

_____

_____

_____

Find an appropriate time to share this information with your partner and invite him or her to let you see his or her map.

List the top three ways your partner spends leisure time. Next identify whether you approve or disapprove of this use of time and why.

_____

_____

_____

_____

_____

_____

_____

Remember to bring completed worksheet to your next appointment.

ACKNOWLEDGMENT

GOALS OF THE EXERCISE

1. To move couples from blaming and misunderstanding one another into listening to and acknowledging their partner's feelings and points of view.
2. To give each person an experience of being heard.

TYPES OF PROBLEMS THIS EXERCISE MAY BE MOST USEFUL FOR

- Blame
- Communication
- Jealousy
- Life-Changing Events
- Midlife Crisis
- Religion/Spirituality Differences
- Work/Home Role Strain

SUGGESTIONS FOR PROCESSING THIS EXERCISE WITH THE COUPLE

1. How was being acknowledged different from your usual conversations or interactions?
2. What did each of you learn from this exercise?
3. What do you plan to do differently in the future because you have done this exercise?

ACKNOWLEDGMENT

Often when conversations get stuck, it's because both participants are paying more attention to getting their own message across than listening. Messages that are sent out but never acknowledged tend to get repeated and repeated louder and faster. Simply acknowledging the point the other is making lets him or her know that you were listening and increases the chance of listening on the part of the other.

At least once a day, repeat the feeling or point of view that your partner is telling you before you express your point. Keep restating it until the partner agrees that you have correctly reflected what is going on. You might want to use the phrase "Let me make sure I understand you" or "So, you're saying … ." Record your results here. Copy this sheet to add more days.

Day 1

What point did you acknowledge?

_____

_____

What was the result of your action?

_____

_____

Day 2

What point did you acknowledge?

_____

_____

What was the result of your action?

_____

_____

Remember to bring completed worksheet to your next appointment.

CATCH YOUR PARTNER DOING SOMETHING RIGHT

GOALS OF THE EXERCISE

1. To change the couple's patterns of attention and talk from blame to praise and credit.
2. To give you, the therapist, information about what is going well in the couple's relationship.

TYPES OF PROBLEMS THIS EXERCISE MAY BE MOST USEFUL FOR

- Anger
- Blame
- Blended-Family Problems
- Communication
- Financial Conflict
- Job Stress
- Sexual Dysfunction
- Work/Home Role Strain

SUGGESTIONS FOR PROCESSING THIS EXERCISE WITH THE COUPLE

1. How did your partner respond when you gave him or her credit?
2. What surprised you about his or her response to getting credit?
3. How will this change your interactions or relationship?

CATCH YOUR PARTNER DOING SOMETHING RIGHT

Most of us are good at noticing when our partner does something we don't like and yet what they "do right" goes unnoticed and unacknowledged. Letting others know when we like what they do is a way of positively reinforcing their behavior as well as teaching them our preferences. This exercise will help you develop your ability to be aware of your partner's efforts.

Between now and your next session (at least twice a day), make a note of something your partner does that you appreciate, that helps your relationship, or that moves things in a positive direction. When possible, find an appropriate way to let your partner know that you appreciate the effort. Watch for times when you felt cared about, helped, or understood, and try to identify specific things that led you to feel that way. (*Hint:* You can also catch yourself doing something right and silently give yourself credit. Notice when you are being flexible, compassionate, and understanding.) Record what you acknowledged and the response of your partner.

Day 1

What did you acknowledge or give your partner credit for?

_____

How did your partner respond?

_____

Day 2

What did you acknowledge or give your partner credit for?

_____

How did your partner respond?

_____

Day 3

What did you acknowledge or give your partner credit for?

_____

How did your partner respond?

_____

Day 4

What did you acknowledge or give your partner credit for?

_____

How did your partner respond?

_____

Day 5

What did you acknowledge or give your partner credit for?

_____

How did your partner respond?

_____

Day 6

What did you acknowledge or give your partner credit for?

_____

How did your partner respond?

_____

Day 7

What did you acknowledge or give your partner credit for?

_____

How did your partner respond?

_____

Remember to bring completed worksheet to your next appointment.

LET YOUR PARTNER KNOW WHAT BEHAVIORS YOU'D LIKE

GOALS OF THE EXERCISE

1. To get couples to begin to focus on what they want rather than what they don't want.
2. To move the discussion into action talk and away from blaming or vague talk.

TYPES OF PROBLEMS THIS EXERCISE MAY BE MOST USEFUL FOR

- Anger
- Blame
- Communication
- Dependency
- Depression
- Jealousy
- Life-Changing Events
- Sexual Dysfunction

SUGGESTIONS FOR PROCESSING THIS EXERCISE WITH THE COUPLE

1. Did anything change as a result of your doing this exercise?
2. Did you discuss your list with your partner?
3. What did you learn from doing this exercise?

LET YOUR PARTNER KNOW WHAT BEHAVIORS YOU'D LIKE

It is easy to complain or identify things we don't like. We often focus on what's not working to the detriment of what we would like to have happening. Identifying and asking for actions that you'd like the other person to start doing or do more of can have a dramatic effect on behavior, especially in situations that involve others. Remember to focus on actions the other person could do, not on changes to their personality or on asking them to give up or alter their feelings.

Make a list of at least three actions relevant to the problem you are working on that you would like the other person to start doing or do more often. Be as specific and clear as possible. Direct your attention to *actions* rather than personality traits or characteristics. You may want to think in terms of small steps in the right direction. Add to your list as time passes between now and your next session. For your next session, be prepared to discuss how you might best use this information.

_____
_____
_____
_____
_____
_____
_____
_____
_____

Remember to bring completed worksheet to your next appointment.

JUST THE FACTS, MA'AM

GOALS OF THE EXERCISE

1. To help couples separate their interpretations and projections from what is actually happening in the relationship.
2. To get couples talking about their interpretations and checking them out with one another.

TYPES OF PROBLEMS THIS EXERCISE MAY BE MOST USEFUL FOR

- Anger
- Blame
- Communication
- Intolerance
- Jealousy
- Loss of Love/Affection

SUGGESTIONS FOR PROCESSING THIS EXERCISE WITH THE COUPLE

1. What surprised you most about your partner's interpretations and stories?
2. Did you notice any patterns in your stories?
3. If so, where, when, or how do you think these patterns arose?

JUST THE FACTS, MA'AM

We all interpret and create stories about the events we experience. These stories often shape our responses to events and situations. Sometimes the stories we make are not helpful and are even the source of problems. One of the ways to challenge unhelpful stories is to separate one's story (interpretation) from what is actually happening (the facts, what you can see and hear). This is one way that you can be open to a new story or just stop getting stuck with the same unhelpful story.

Think of a situation that you are unhappy about in your relationship. Describe what happens as if you could see it on a videotape or as if you were telling it to Sergeant Joe Friday, who just wanted the facts—not interpretation or feelings, just the facts.

_____

_____

Now list the reasons why you think the other person did what he or she did or what it means that these things happened in your relationship. Aspects of stories we typically use:

Intentions: What do you think your partner was trying to accomplish by doing the behavior?

Traits: What traits or characteristics do you think your partner was showing when doing the behavior?

The Past: What link to the past does this behavior have?

The Future: What does this say to you about the likely future of your relationship?

_____

_____

_____

The answers to these questions are the stories; they may be factual or they may be your own interpretations. Either way, it is good to check them out with your partner and not automatically assume they are true. You may find that you can put your stories on the back burner and deal only with the facts. Use another sheet of paper if you need more room.

Remember to bring completed worksheet to your next appointment.

MAP THE PROBLEM

GOALS OF THE EXERCISE

1. To get couples to gather objective information for the therapist about the typical course and pattern of the problem.
2. To locate places to intervene in the pattern to change the problem.

TYPES OF PROBLEMS THIS EXERCISE MAY BE MOST USEFUL FOR

- Alcohol Abuse
- Anger
- Dependency
- Depression
- Eating Disorder
- Physical Abuse
- Psychological Abuse

SUGGESTIONS FOR PROCESSING THIS EXERCISE WITH THE COUPLE

1. Did you find that while you were gathering information about the problem, you came up with some ideas about how to change it?
2. What is one thing that each of you could do differently now that you have learned about the typical pattern of the problem?
3. If you were an engineer, could you redesign this problem so that it would lead to a solution or a better outcome?

MAP THE PROBLEM

This is an exercise in observation, both of yourself and your partner in a problem situation. Between now and your next session, observe yourself and your partner when a problem happens. Spell out as specifically as possible what typically happens when the problem occurs. The more details you include, the more helpful this exercise is likely to be. Take notes as the problem unfolds if you need to. It would be helpful for each person to do this exercise independently.

1. When does the problem usually happen?

    _____

    _____

2. When does the problem rarely happen?

    _____

    _____

3. Where does the problem usually happen?

    _____

    _____

4. Where does the problem rarely happen?

    _____

    _____

5. Are there any other constants you can identify about when the problem happens and when it doesn't?

    _____

    _____

6. What is your first inkling that the problem is starting? Be specific about words, body language, actions, and voice.

    _____

    _____

7.   How do you respond? Be specific about words, body language, actions, and voice.

_____

_____

8.   What does your partner do? Be specific about words, body language, actions, and voice.

_____

_____

Write a detailed step-by-step account or draw a flowchart of how the problem typically unfolds. Use another sheet of paper if necessary.

Remember to bring completed worksheet to your next appointment.

BREAKING PATTERNS

GOALS OF THE EXERCISE

1. To suggest that couples have some control over their situation.
2. To introduce some change into the situation.
3. To dissuade couples from attempting to change everything at once.

TYPES OF PROBLEMS THIS EXERCISE MAY BE MOST USEFUL FOR

- Alcohol Abuse
- Anger
- Blame
- Dependency
- Depression
- Eating Disorder
- Physical Abuse
- Psychological Abuse

SUGGESTIONS FOR PROCESSING THIS EXERCISE WITH THE COUPLE

1. What do you want to change?
2. What is it that you would rather be doing?
3. What did you learn by keeping your old behavior?
4. What did you learn on the days you tried something different?
5. What difference will this make?

BREAKING PATTERNS

One of the handy things that the human brain is able to do is to learn behaviors that can be used over and over. While this ability is great most of the time, it sometimes works against us. If you have learned a behavior pattern that no longer works and is causing you distress, you can often break away from it by using humor. Lighten up and get silly. For instance, instead of fighting, get water pistols, stand back to back, and walk out 10 paces in opposite directions; then turn and fire until the water pistols are empty. Have a water balloon fight or a pillow fight (light pillows or boppers).

Describe what you will do to break the pattern the next time you notice it.

_____

_____

After you have broken the pattern, answer the following questions:

Who noticed the pattern, and what did you notice?

_____

_____

What would have happened if you had not done the exercise?

_____

_____

How did the exercise change things?

_____

_____

What did you learn from this that you can use in the future?

_____

_____

Remember to bring completed worksheet to your next appointment.

DON'T GET EVEN, GET ODD

GOALS OF THE EXERCISE

1. To suggest that the client has some control over the situation.
2. To introduce some change into the situation.
3. To dissuade the client from changing everything at once.

TYPES OF PROBLEMS THIS EXERCISE MAY BE MOST USEFUL FOR

- Anger
- Anxiety
- Blame
- Blended-Family Problems
- Communication
- Dependency
- Depression Due to Relationship
- Depression Independent of Relationship Problems
- Work/Home Role Strain

SUGGESTIONS FOR PROCESSING THIS EXERCISE WITH THE COUPLE

1. What do you want to change?
2. What is it that you would rather be doing?
3. What did you learn by keeping your old behavior?
4. What did you learn on the days you tried something different?
5. What difference will this make?

DON'T GET EVEN, GET ODD

Sometimes when change is difficult, it can be helpful to learn a bit more about a behavior before changing it. Here is one way to do that.

Write clearly the behavior you want to change.

_____

_____

_____

_____

What would you rather be doing?

_____

_____

_____

_____

On even-numbered days (for example, the second and fourth of the month), do nothing different. Make those days exactly like the days you have been having. On odd-numbered days, do the new behavior. For each day, answer the questions:

Odd Day 1: What did you do that was the same old thing?

Observations and Comments:

_____

_____

_____

Even Day 1: What did you do that was different?

Observations and Comments:

_____

_____

_____

Odd Day 2: What did you do that was the same old thing?

Observations and Comments:

_____

_____

_____

Even Day 2: What did you do that was different?

Observations and Comments:

_____

_____

_____

Odd Day 3: What did you do that was the same old thing?

Observations and Comments:

_____

_____

_____

Even Day 3: What did you do that was different?

Observations and Comments:

_____

_____

_____

Odd Day 4: What did you do that was the same old thing?

Observations and Comments:

_____

_____

_____

Even Day 4: What did you do that was different?

Observations and Comments:

_____

_____

_____

Odd Day 5: What did you do that was the same old thing?
Observations and Comments:

_____

_____

_____

Even Day 5: What did you do that was different?
Observations and Comments:

_____

_____

_____

Odd Day 6: What did you do that was the same old thing?
Observations and Comments:

_____

_____

_____

Even Day 6: What did you do that was different?
Observations and Comments:

_____

_____

_____

Odd Day 7: What did you do that was the same old thing?
Observations and Comments:

_____

_____

_____

Even Day 7: What did you do that was different?
Observations and Comments:

_____

_____

_____

Remember to bring completed worksheet to your next appointment.

CHANGE THE CONTEXT

GOALS OF THE EXERCISE

1. To give clients a sense that they can make a difference in their problem.
2. To raise awareness of spiritual and family/cultural background options and resources.

TYPES OF PROBLEMS THIS EXERCISE MAY BE MOST USEFUL FOR

- Blended-Family Problems
- Recreational Activities Disputes
- Religion/Spirituality Differences

SUGGESTIONS FOR PROCESSING THIS EXERCISE WITH THE COUPLE

1. Which one of these suggestions appealed to you the most? Why?
2. What changes came from doing this exercise?
3. Can you think of other things that weren't suggested in the exercise that are like the suggestions given here and that might be helpful?

CHANGE THE CONTEXT

Sometimes trying to directly change the situation leads to resistance and frustration. Coming through the side door, rather than taking a frontal approach, can lead to better results. In this exercise, we suggest you try changing anything that is in the context around the problem.

Possibilities include changing the timing of the problem, changing where it usually takes place, drawing on your spiritual resources, challenging your usual gender training (for example, women usually wait until the other person is done talking to speak, but men often interrupt). Here we provide a list of some of the variables and taken-for-granted aspects of your context that you could question, challenge, and change. Pick any of these that appeal to you and try them in the next week.

1. Notice and change the usual timing of the problem, that is, when it usually happens, how long it lasts, or its frequency. You might time your arguments and limit them to five minutes each. Take a break for five minutes and then start again for another five minutes. If you usually argue at night, make time in the early morning hours to argue. Record your actions and the results.

    _____

    _____

    _____

2. Change the usual location for the problem or the spatial arrangement of your arguments or problems. One couple who couldn't stop arguing went into the bathroom. The man lay down in the bathtub and the woman sat on the toilet next to the bathtub. They ended up feeling so strange that they changed their arguing styles and were able to sort things out much better. Record your actions and the results.

    _____

    _____

    _____

3. Identify your usual conflict patterns that you learned from the family in which you grew up, and try some new ones. Some families never argue or raise their voices. Some families argue all the time and always raise their voices. Ask three of your friends to teach you the conflict resolution or avoidance patterns they learned from their families and practice using them in your relationship. Record your actions and the results.

_____

_____

_____

4. In the middle of a conflict, get in touch with your spirituality in whatever way you are comfortable (praying, believing that each person is a child of God, imagining your connection to universal love, having a sense that Jesus, Mohammed, Allah, Zoroaster, or Buddha is in the room with you). Proceed with the conflict with your spiritual resources leading the way. Record your actions and the results.

_____

_____

_____

Remember to bring completed worksheet to your next appointment.

NEGOTIATING IMPASSES

GOALS OF THE EXERCISE

1. To help couples learn or use negotiation skills.
2. To get couples through an impasse.

TYPES OF PROBLEMS THIS EXERCISE MAY BE MOST USEFUL FOR

- Blame
- Communication
- Personality Differences

SUGGESTIONS FOR PROCESSING THIS EXERCISE WITH THE COUPLE

1. Which method for negotiation appealed the most to each of you?
2. Which were you able to use?
3. Can you think of other issues it might be good to use any of these methods with?

NEGOTIATING IMPASSES

When you come to loggerheads, sometimes it seems as though there is no solution. Try one of these four methods for negotiating differences or impasses. Try them in the spirit of experimentation. They may not solve the problem (or they might), but they might get you unstuck from your impasse.

1. Take turns doing it one partner's way and then the other's for an agreed-upon period of time. For example, one person wants to buy takeout on his or her night to cook and the other would rather have a home-cooked meal. For one month, try takeout food. For the next month, try home-cooked meals. Check in with your partner after two months and discuss the results of the experiment.

2. Split the difference. For example, if you want to go out to eat every weekend and your partner wants to go out only once per month, go out twice per month. If one of you wants to ground your teenager for a month for coming home late and the other thinks it should be for one night, try grounding your child for a week or every weekend for a month.

3. Find another action that would represent a show of good faith to your partner rather than the one he or she is demanding. For example, if your partner wants you to take dancing lessons and you are unwilling, your partner may conclude that you are unwilling to try anything new. Find some other activity besides dancing that he or she would also like to do that you would agree to do that would show your partner that you are willing to try something new.

4. Drop the issue for a time and focus on areas in which both of you can agree and are willing to change. Agree that you will take up this tough issue again, say in a month or six months, but for now, let it go. Time sometimes brings new perspectives or new circumstances that allow for a solution.

GO APE

GOALS OF THE EXERCISE

1. To get couples out of their usual ways of interacting.
2. To access creative and nonverbal ways of communicating and interacting.

TYPES OF PROBLEMS THIS EXERCISE MAY BE MOST USEFUL FOR

- Anger
- Blame
- Communication
- Dependency
- Jealousy
- Midlife Crisis
- Sexual Dysfunction
- Work/Home Role Strain

SUGGESTIONS FOR PROCESSING THIS EXERCISE WITH THE COUPLE

1. How did this exercise feel for each of you?
2. What surprised you the most about this way of arguing?
3. Can you think of other ways in which "going ape" might be helpful in your relationship?

GO APE

Unique problems call for unique solutions.

Between now and your next session, whenever you begin to argue, initiate two rules:

1. You may use only those communication methods that apes would have (hugs, grunts, pantomime, etc.).

2. No violence.

When you are finished, answer the following questions:

What was hard about this exercise?

_____

_____

_____

Explain three ways this argument was different from those you have had in the past.

_____

_____

_____

What are three things about arguing this way that are better than the way you have been doing it?

_____

_____

_____

List three things you learned from doing this exercise.

_____

_____

_____

How can you use this information in the future?

_____

_____

_____

Remember to bring completed worksheet to your next appointment.

LETTER TO THE PROBLEM

GOALS OF THE EXERCISE

1. To externalize the problem.
2. To join clients.
3. To encourage acceptance and acknowledgment of feelings.

TYPES OF PROBLEMS THIS EXERCISE MAY BE MOST USEFUL FOR

- Addictions
- Eating Disorder
- Illness
- Mental Illness
- Personality Differences

SUGGESTIONS FOR PROCESSING THIS EXERCISE WITH THE COUPLE

1. How did this exercise change the way you think about the problem?
2. What did you learn that might be helpful in dealing with the problem?
3. What was it like being the problem?

LETTER TO THE PROBLEM

1. Write a joint letter from the two of you to your problem. You could include:
   - How you see the situation
   - Your feelings about the problem
   - What you want from the problem
   - Consequences of not getting what you want
   - Anything else you like

2. Imagine that you are the problem and write a response to the issues raised in the letter.

3. Write another joint letter to the problem in answer to what the problem has told you.

4. How did your first and second letters to the problem differ?

   _____

   _____

   _____

   _____

5. What did you learn from this exercise?

   _____

   _____

   _____

   _____

   _____

Remember to bring completed worksheet to your next appointment.

GOING POSTAL INSTEAD OF GOING POSTAL

GOALS OF THE EXERCISE

1. To suggest a safe way to express feelings.
2. To acknowledge each partner's right to his or her feelings.

TYPES OF PROBLEMS THIS EXERCISE MAY BE MOST USEFUL FOR

- Anger
- Blame
- Communication
- Intolerance
- Jealousy
- Loss of Love/Affection

SUGGESTIONS FOR PROCESSING THIS EXERCISE WITH THE COUPLE

1. Allow each partner to discuss the contents of the letter to the extent that he or she thinks it is helpful.
2. What do you want to do with the letter?
3. Will this be the last such letter you will write?

GOING POSTAL INSTEAD OF GOING POSTAL

Sometimes we don't resolve an issue at the time that it arises. It might be something from childhood or from an earlier relationship. Frequently, such an issue can be satisfactorily reopened and resolved. This exercise presents one way to do that.

Write a letter to a person with whom you feel you have unfinished business. Use this sheet to get your thoughts together; then write the letter.

- Write a factual account of the situation that caused the problem.

  _____

  _____

- What haven't you said?

  _____

  _____

- Explain your feelings about the problem.

  _____

  _____

- What do you appreciate about what happened?

  _____

  _____

- What do you not appreciate about what happened?

  _____

  _____

- List any regrets you have about the situation.

  _____

  _____

- Spell out clearly any wishes, demands, or requests you want to make.

  _____

  _____

• Is there anything else you want to include in the letter?

_____

_____

After you have composed the letter, answer the following questions:

• What do you want to do with the letter?

_____

_____

• If it can't be delivered or if it is better for you not to do so, list three things that you could do with the letter that might be meaningful to you.

_____

_____

Remember to bring completed worksheet to your next appointment.

LIGHTEN YOUR LOAD

GOALS OF THE EXERCISE

1. To physically represent some unfinished emotion or situation for one or both of the partners.
2. To help clients to finish or let go of unfinished business.

TYPES OF PROBLEMS THIS EXERCISE MAY BE MOST USEFUL FOR

- Betrayal
- Infidelity
- Jealousy
- Loss of Love/Affection
- Sexual Dysfunction

SUGGESTIONS FOR PROCESSING THIS EXERCISE WITH THE COUPLE

1. How did this exercise affect your feelings about the unfinished or problem situation?
2. Are there any other issues that you think it would be helpful to use this exercise with?
3. How was it not to talk about the problem with your partner?

LIGHTEN YOUR LOAD

Sometimes we dwell on problems that can't be easily resolved or perhaps will never be resolved. If you are dwelling on a problem as an individual or as a couple, here's an idea for getting the problem out of your mind.

Write down the name of the person, the emotion, or the unresolved situation on a piece of paper. Carry it around with you (or both of you carry a copy) for as long as you need to feel as if the paper is now connected to the problem or unfinished business. Then decide on your own or talk over as a couple a place you might leave the piece of paper in order to symbolically leave the problem behind. It might be under a rock; it might be at someone's grave; it might be flushed down the toilet or thrown into the ocean. Choose a special time (an anniversary of some event, a birthday, or a holiday, such as Independence Day) to get rid of your piece of paper. Make a note on your calendar to have a conversation one month after you do this.

Don't mention the problem to your partner for one month. At the end of that time, sit down and write three things that have changed for each of you since you got rid of the paper.

_____

_____

_____

_____

_____

_____

_____

_____

Remember to bring completed worksheet to your next appointment.

CAN DO!

GOALS OF THE EXERCISE

1. To interrupt the usual pattern of conflict between the partners.
2. To externalize the problems and help each partner let some issues go.

TYPES OF PROBLEMS THIS EXERCISE MAY BE MOST USEFUL FOR

- Anger
- Blame
- Communication
- Financial Conflict
- Job Stress
- Work/Home Role Strain

SUGGESTIONS FOR PROCESSING THIS EXERCISE WITH THE COUPLE

1. How did you let go of the problems that you did discard?
2. What did you learn from doing this exercise?
3. How did it feel to delay when you usually deal with things much more quickly?

CAN DO!

We all know that we can't change the past. In spite of that, it's common for people to bring up old problems while trying to solve new ones. This can be destructive and frustrating. Whenever you find yourself revisiting an old injustice, write it on a piece of paper and put it in a can on the top shelf of your kitchen cabinet. Once a month, pull out the can and go through the papers. Decide which memories you want to continue to maintain. Get rid of those that you don't need to hold on to. When you feel the urge to discuss the past, remember that you have it in a can where it won't be forgotten until you are ready to give it your full attention.

How many old problems did you collect?

_____

_____

_____

How many did you discard?

_____

_____

_____

How did you decide which ones to discard?

_____

_____

_____

How did you get rid of them?

_____

_____

_____

Remember to bring completed worksheet to your next appointment.

PLANT A TREE

GOALS OF THE EXERCISE

1. To help couples find a physical way of representing some significant experience.
2. To give the message that life is always moving, as are grief, joy, and people's developmental lives.

TYPES OF PROBLEMS THIS EXERCISE MAY BE MOST USEFUL FOR

- Life-Changing Event
- Midlife Crisis

SUGGESTIONS FOR PROCESSING THIS EXERCISE WITH THE COUPLE

1. What was your experience with this exercise?
2. What advice would you now give others who are facing issues similar to those you were facing when you did this exercise?
3. What did you learn about yourself in the choices you made designing this tree-planting ritual?

PLANT A TREE

The old tradition of marking important dates by planting a tree has been largely lost in our urban society. In the past, people planted trees to mark births, deaths, anniversaries, and other important events. You may find it helpful to revive this old tradition and create your own ritual around it. This type of ritual can have unexpected benefits for years as you watch the tree grow.

Take some time to think about the following questions. If appropriate, include friends and family in the planning.

Who do you want to be present?

_____

_____

What kind of tree is most appropriate?

_____

_____

Who will dig the hole and plant the tree?

_____

_____

What would you want said and by whom? You may want to include prayers, poems, or music (or perhaps silence).

_____

_____

Would you like to put anything in the hole with the tree?

_____

_____

Do you want to include a meal or refreshments? If so, what?

_____

_____

Is there anything else that you would like to include?

_____

_____

Remember to bring completed worksheet to your next appointment.

TIMEOUT HANDOUT

GOALS OF THE EXERCISE

1.　To develop solution-building interactions.
2.　To reduce emotionality.

TYPES OF PROBLEMS THIS EXERCISE MAY BE MOST USEFUL FOR

- Abuse
- Bullying

SUGGESTIONS FOR PROCESSING THIS EXERCISE WITH THE COUPLE

1.　Frame timeout as a success at breaking an unwanted pattern.
2.　Offer encouragement for any success using timeouts.
3.　Review the process used to identify the proper time for timeout.
4.　Explore any difficulties or reluctance to take a timeout.
5.　Explore the clients' opinions about the usefulness of this exercise.

TIMEOUT HANDOUT

It is commonly recognized that extreme emotions interfere with clear thinking. Venting anger can cause more problems than it solves. If you have found this to be true, you may want to try interrupting a discussion when negative emotions begin to take over. Take enough time to calm yourself (usually fifteen or twenty minutes is enough), then try again. Here are some suggestions for what to think about during your timeout.

1. Congratulate yourself for taking a timeout. You just took a step toward breaking an old habit that wasn't working.

2. Take a few deep breaths and allow yourself to calm down if you need to. Take a walk or do something physical if necessary.

3. Define for yourself the point of disagreement.
    *   Is it an issue you can ignore?
    *   Is it something that isn't so important itself but is an example of a larger issue? If so, talk about that issue.

4. Clearly define what you want; then ask for it. Why is it important to you?

Things to remember:

*   Don't try to defeat your partner, but at the same time, try not to lose. If anyone loses, your relationship suffers. Rather, look for a solution you can both live with.

*   Try to turn the discussion into a problem-solving exercise rather than a win-lose contest.

*   Stick to the facts—things you can see, hear, and touch.

*   You can call another timeout.

*   Listen until you understand how your partner is thinking. Check it out to be sure.

*   Leave yourself open to be influenced.

ANGER LOG

GOALS OF THE EXERCISE

1. To encourage deconstruction of the experience of anger.
2. To encourage self-awareness.
3. To identify places to interrupt destructive patterns.

TYPES OF PROBLEMS THIS EXERCISE MAY BE MOST USEFUL FOR

- Abuse
- Bullying

SUGGESTIONS FOR PROCESSING THIS EXERCISE WITH THE COUPLE

1. Identify patterns and make them conscious.
2. What have you learned about situations that may cause problems for you?
3. How do you know you are getting angry? Physical sensation? Certain thoughts?

ANGER LOG

The onset of anger can feel out of control. By studying your experience and patterns with anger, you can take control by identifying moments and opportunities to act differently.

Date: _____   Time: _____

    What happened before you got angry? _____

    I was angry about: _____

    On a 1-to-10 scale from calm to outraged, I would rate my anger this time at: _____

    Triggers: I know I was angry because: _____

    _____

    What I did: _____

    _____

    What I like about what I did: _____

    _____

    What I wish I had done differently: _____

    _____

Date: _____   Time: _____

    What happened before you got angry? _____

    I was angry about: _____

    On a 1-to-10 scale from calm to outraged, I would rate my anger this time at: _____

    Triggers: I know I was angry because: _____

    _____

    What I did: _____

    _____

    What I like about what I did: _____

    _____

    What I wish I had done differently: _____

    _____

Remember to bring completed worksheet to your next appointment.

SETTING BOUNDARIES

GOALS OF THE EXERCISE

1. To encourage communication about difficult subjects.
2. To simplify messages.
3. To raise important issues.

TYPES OF PROBLEMS THIS EXERCISE MAY BE MOST USEFUL FOR

- Communication Issues
- Dissatisfaction without Clear Definition of the Problem
- Premarriage Counseling

SUGGESTIONS FOR PROCESSING THIS EXERCISE WITH THE COUPLE

1. Review the answers in the session.
2. Explore the personal meaning behind the boundary (e.g., "What does it mean to you that she wants e-mail kept private?").
3. Are both partners willing to do what they are requesting of each other? If not, what's that about?

SETTING BOUNDARIES

Every couple must define their own line of separation between individual and partner. If left undefined, this boundary is almost guaranteed to cause problems.

Here is a list of things that people often disagree about. For this exercise, both of you independently indicate which behaviors you are comfortable with and which you are not. Then share your answers and practice your negotiation skills.

Enter the bathroom without knocking.	OK	No way
Use my toiletries, nail clippers, toothbrush, etc.	OK	No way
Tell me what to wear without an invitation to do so.	OK	No way
Look through my clothes drawers/closet.	OK	No way
Pick my friends.	OK	No way
Look through my billfold or purse.	OK	No way
Ask me, "Who was that and what did you talk about?" after a phone call.	OK	No way
Ask where I'm going or when I'll be back.	OK	No way
Talk about me with family when I'm not there.	OK	No way
Wear my clothes.	OK	No way
Look into my cell phone call history and address book.	OK	No way
Read my diary or other writings.	OK	No way
Read my e-mail or check my browsing history.	OK	No way
Track my movements (e.g., following, GPS, phone calls).	OK	No way
Tell me how to manage my health.	OK	No way
Have lunch with member of the opposite sex.	OK	No way
Have drinks with member of the opposite sex.	OK	No way
Have friends of the opposite sex.	OK	No way
Talk on the phone with member of the opposite sex.	OK	No way

Have dinner with member of the opposite sex.   OK   No way

Say negative things about my family.   OK   No way

Sexual relationship with member of same sex.   OK   No way

Sexual relationship with member of opposite sex.   OK   No way

Add any other things you think you might need to negotiate.

_____

_____

_____

_____

_____

Remember to bring completed worksheet to your next appointment.

BIODOTS

GOAL OF THE EXERCISE

1. To make couples more aware of their stress levels so they can make choices about the most and least beneficial times to have a conversation.

TYPES OF PROBLEMS THIS EXERCISE MAY BE MOST USEFUL FOR

- Anger Management
- Bullying or Verbal Abuse
- Conflict
- Stress

SUGGESTIONS FOR PROCESSING THIS EXERCISE WITH THE COUPLE

1. How did you decide when to use the dots?
2. What did you notice that would make you aware of being stressed even without the dots?
3. How did you calm yourself?
4. Did the presence of the biodots change your behavior? How? How can you use that knowledge even when you aren't using the biodots?

BIODOTS

Research shows that when we are stressed our communication skills are at their worst. We do not listen or process information as effectively, let alone articulate our thoughts and intentions. Yet what is said during a fight or tense conversation is sometimes presumed to be our partner's true thoughts and feelings. Many critical conversations occur when one or both partners are their most relationally impaired. This exercise is intended to help couples identify their stress levels and choose the most effective times to communicate.

When you are starting to have a stressful conversation, pull out the biodots.* If the biodot is black, take a break and calm down. Take some time apart or try the following relaxation technique: Breathe deeply into your lower abdomen for a count of five and then exhale through your nose for a count of two. Repeat this until the biodot shows that you are calm.

---

*Biodots are available online from Biodots of Indiana or by phone at 1-800-272-2340. Biodots are small circles of micro-encapsulated liquid crystals that gauge changes in skin temperature and change color to indicate the temperature level. The more stressed you are, the cooler your skin temperature; the more relaxed you are, the warmer your skin. (When you are stressed, your blood tends to pool more toward your central vital organs; thus your hands become cooler.) Biodots come with a card that identifies what the various colors mean. Usually black or dark purple indicates stress.

BREATHING

GOAL OF THE EXERCISE

1. To help couples connect in an intimate, nonsexual way.

TYPES OF PROBLEMS THIS EXERCISE MAY BE MOST USEFUL FOR

- Conflict
- Couples with Sexual Issues
- Dual-Career Couples
- Nonsexual Couples
- Parents
- Rebuilding Trust
- Stress

SUGGESTIONS FOR PROCESSING THIS EXERCISE WITH THE COUPLE

1. What did you notice?
2. Which felt better or more comfortable?
3. Was doing the exercise helpful?
4. Would it be helpful to do this regularly or at particular times?
5. Are there ways to make it more useful?

BREATHING

Given busy lives and multiple demands, it can require some effort to maintain an intimate connection with our partners. This exercise can help couples ground and reconnect.

For this exercise, you and your partner sit back-to-back on the floor. Without speaking, spend three to five minutes feeling the rhythm of each other's breathing.

Next, without speaking, attempt to coordinate breathing so that you and your partner breathe in and out at the same time.

Variations:

Try the exercise while having an intimate conversation.

Try it while having a challenging conversation.

Think about any of the minute frustrations that result from living with another person, and let go of them.

Tell your partner what you most enjoy about him or her and your relationship.

LET'S GET PHYSICAL

GOAL OF THE EXERCISE

1. To help clients renew or develop a physical connection.

TYPES OF PROBLEMS THIS EXERCISE MAY BE MOST USEFUL FOR

- Conflict
- Couples with Sexual Issues
- Dual-Career Couples
- Nonsexual Couples
- Parents
- Rebuilding Trust
- Stress

SUGGESTIONS FOR PROCESSING THIS EXERCISE WITH THE COUPLE

1. What did you notice?
2. Which activity felt better or more comfortable?
3. Was doing the exercise helpful?
4. Would it be helpful to do this more frequently?
5. Are there ways to make it more useful?

LET'S GET PHYSICAL

We may be dating ourselves, but do you remember Olivia Newton-John singing, "Let's get physical, physical. Let me hear your body talk, your body talk"? Relationship interactions are based on a variety of elements—kinesthetic, visual, auditory, emotional, and so on. As life gets busy or there is any kind of relationship strain, the first thing that goes is usually physical contact. Research has confirmed the importance of touch for physical and emotional well-being. This homework assignment is asking you to incorporate activities that promote touch and physical intimacy.

Pick an activity from the following list or add your own.

Dance (ballroom, tango, salsa, etc.).

Ride a motorcycle together.

Walk and hold hands.

Engage in couples yoga.

Engage in couples massage.

Massage each other.

Sit next to each other at a restaurant.

Hold hands at the movies.

Snuggle.

Participate in at least several activities a week that require you to be physically intimate.

VALUE YOUR DIFFERENCES

GOALS OF THE EXERCISE

1. To help couples understand their differences.
2. To help couples appreciate their different values.

TYPES OF PROBLEMS THIS EXERCISE MAY BE MOST USEFUL FOR

- Communication Issues
- Life-Changing Events
- Religion/Spirituality Differences

SUGGESTIONS FOR PROCESSING THIS EXERCISE WITH THE COUPLE

1. What surprised you about your partner's values or differences compared to your ways of thinking about situations?
2. In what areas did you have similar or the same values or perceptions?
3. How will doing this exercise help you in the future?

VALUE YOUR DIFFERENCES

It's easy to say that having different kinds of people in the world keeps things from getting boring, but it's quite another thing to live with some of those people. Learning to value differences in others is a challenge for most of us. Often we assume that everyone, especially our partner, has the same values, motivations, and ways of understanding the world that we do. If others act in a way that upsets us or perplexes us, usually that indicates that they have a different understanding or perspective from ours. There are several ways to value differences rather than have them be sources of conflict or hurt. The first is to be genuinely curious about how the other person makes sense of what he or she did.

Each day for the next week, keep notes on a way that your partner is different from you or acts differently than you would. Ask your partner to explain how he or she understood the situation. Do not criticize or judge the person or the explanation. Just try to put yourself in your partner's shoes and understand how he or she could see things in that light or with those values.

Explain to your partner how you understood or thought about that same situation differently. Again, do not try to convince the other person that your way is right and his or hers is wrong. Just communicate your way of making sense of the situation.

The Buddhists believe that our differences are great opportunities to learn. For each difference, note at least one way or context in which your partner's viewpoint or behavior could be valuable.

Remember to bring completed worksheet to your next appointment.

ACCOUNTABILITY

GOALS OF THE EXERCISE

1. To help couples recognize places where they have not been accountable.
2. To help couples develop accountability.

TYPES OF PROBLEMS THIS EXERCISE MAY BE MOST USEFUL FOR

- Blame
- Depression Due to Relationship Problems
- Financial Conflict
- Infidelity
- Jealousy
- Physical Abuse
- Psychological Abuse
- Sexual Abuse

SUGGESTIONS FOR PROCESSING THIS EXERCISE WITH THE COUPLE

1. Where did you find holes in your accountability?
2. How did you talk about the situation differently when you spoke about it in an accountable way?
3. How will doing this exercise change your relationship in the future?

ACCOUNTABILITY

Accountability has two components: (1) acknowledging what you did (or do) and (2) not giving excuses or explanations to suggest you couldn't help doing what you did.

Arguments or conflicts can arise when one or both of you are not being accountable for something you do or have done. Instead of being accountable, you divert attention, give excuses, or justify why you couldn't help doing what you did.

Typical excuses or explanations:

Genetic: I've just got this biological/genetic/biochemical nature or condition that makes me act this way.

Developmental: I was raised this way and therefore I have to act this way.

Interpersonal: He made me do it. It was a reaction. If she hadn't nagged me, I wouldn't have hit her.

In this exercise, discuss some behavior that upset your partner and for which you haven't been accountable. Try to reflect an acknowledgment of accountability. Just describe what behavior you did without offering any rationalization or excuse.

_____

_____

_____

_____

_____

_____

_____

_____

Remember to bring completed worksheet to your next appointment.

RESTORING TRUST AND FAITH WHEN ONE PARTNER HAS BETRAYED THE RELATIONSHIP

GOALS OF THE EXERCISE

1. To help repair betrayed trust.
2. To call the partner who betrayed trust to accountability.

TYPES OF PROBLEMS THIS EXERCISE MAY BE MOST USEFUL FOR

- Infidelity
- Jealousy
- Physical Abuse
- Psychological Abuse
- Sexual Abuse

SUGGESTIONS FOR PROCESSING THIS EXERCISE WITH THE COUPLE

1. [To the partner who betrayed] How was it to acknowledge and take responsibility for your actions?
2. [To the partner who was betrayed] How was it to hear your partner acknowledge and take responsibility for the betrayal?
3. How will doing this exercise affect the future of your relationship?

RESTORING TRUST AND FAITH WHEN ONE PARTNER HAS BETRAYED THE RELATIONSHIP

If one of you has violated the boundaries or integrity of the relationship by doing some-thing unethical or harmful (like lying, being unfaithful, spending money you had agreed not to spend, keeping a secret that affected your partner in a negative way, telling a secret that embarrassed or betrayed your partner, etc.), there are steps you could take to restore trust and integrity to your relationship.

1. Take 100% accountability. Acknowledge that you messed up. You could do this in writing or face-to-face. Make sure you don't blame anyone else or offer excuses or reasons that let you off the hook in terms of responsibility. Just describe what you did. The discussion of reasons and extenuating circumstances is usually best left for another time. Write out the facts of the situation and skip the commentary.

2. Offer an apology and ask your partner if there is anything you can do to rectify things. If possible, make amends in the way he or she requests. Note what your partner tells you. Write your own amends plan or contract. Be sure to include a time frame.

3. Make a promise that you won't betray your partner in the future, and follow through with all the actions you have promised. Be scrupulous about your future behavior. Don't allow yourself to be sidetracked. Detail the promises that you have made.

4. If you feel you may be unable to follow through, be forthright and let your partner know before there is a problem.

INEQUITIES

GOALS OF THE EXERCISE

1. To help couples more equitably divide household chores.
2. To raise awareness of inequities in the relationship.

TYPES OF PROBLEMS THIS EXERCISE MAY BE MOST USEFUL FOR

- Job Stress
- Work/Home Role Strain

SUGGESTIONS FOR PROCESSING THIS EXERCISE WITH THE COUPLE

1. Were you surprised by the division of the tasks?
2. What did you learn from doing this exercise?
3. How do you think that the ideas you got from your family of origin and your culture influence how you divide tasks?

INEQUITIES

Having the sense that one is being treated unfairly can be toxic to a relationship. Chores and household responsibilities can be a source of feelings of inequity in a relationship. This exercise can assist in equally distributing household chores. The principle can also be applied to other situations where fairness is an issue.

List all the activities and chores you want to divide:

_____

_____

_____

_____

_____

_____

_____

_____

_____

_____

_____

_____

First divide up the tasks you agree about. Divide the remaining chores into two groups. Let one person divide the chores and the other person choose which group he or she will do. Agree to switch after an agreed-upon period of time (one month, etc.). If you can't decide which person will do the dividing, flip a coin. List the chores, the name of the person who will do each chore, and for what period of time they will do it.

_____

_____

_____

_____

_____

_____

_____

_____

_____

_____

_____

_____

Set a date when you will meet again and renegotiate the current division of labor.

_____

_____

Remember to bring completed worksheet to your next appointment.

FEELING RESPONSIBLE: WHO INITIATES THINGS THAT NEED TO BE DONE

GOALS OF THE EXERCISE

1. To help the couple become aware of inequities in who takes responsibility for and initiates joint tasks.
2. To introduce an awareness and discussion of gender training influences on each partner and the relationship.

TYPES OF PROBLEMS THIS EXERCISE MAY BE MOST USEFUL FOR

- Financial Conflict
- Job Stress
- Parenting Conflict
- Work/Home Role Strain

SUGGESTIONS FOR PROCESSING THIS EXERCISE WITH THE COUPLE

1. Were you aware of this issue before you did this exercise?
2. What ways were you trained as a man or as a woman in the areas of responsibility?
3. Do you agree with this societal programming or are there places where it doesn't fit for you and your relationship?
4. How might you challenge this inequality in feeling responsible?

FEELING RESPONSIBLE: WHO INITIATES THINGS THAT NEED TO BE DONE

Sometimes chores and family and household tasks are divided somewhat equitably, but one person still feels as if he or she (usually she, since we train women in this culture to take responsibility for relationships and other people, as well as household chores) has the burden for making things happen. This may be an issue in your relationship.

Sit down and make a list of all the chores and family and household responsibilities you have as a couple. To help you think about this issue of responsibility, here is a list that you can use to clarify who usually initiates, does, or feels responsible for each item:

- Cleaning the house
- Doing the cooking
- Grocery shopping
- Cleaning up after a meal
- Doing the laundry
- Making doctor's or dentist's appointments for self or others
- Making appointments for getting the car serviced or repaired
- Calling household repair people
- Meeting household repair people when they arrive to do their work
- Noticing that things around the house need repair or servicing
- Compiling the information for tax preparation
- Paying the bills
- Making a budget
- Making money
- Coordinating children's school and after-school activities
- Caring for the children
- Arranging for childcare when neither parent is available
- Making social arrangements
- Driving or arranging transportation for children to activities, school, or friends

- Arranging or planning vacations
- Doing yardwork
- Calling friends or relatives to stay in touch
- Writing friends or relatives to stay in touch
- Buying Christmas, Hanukkah, Kwanzaa, birthday, or other special occasion cards
- Shopping for clothing
- Maintaining clothing (doing laundry, dropping off/picking up dry cleaning, ironing, replacing buttons, mending, etc.)
- Helping children with homework
- Writing or sending special occasion cards
- _____
- _____
- _____
- _____
- _____

Is there an imbalance in who usually takes responsibility for these tasks? If so, have the partner who usually takes less responsibility agree to take on three of the tasks the other partner usually takes responsibility for during the next month. List those three tasks:

_____

_____

_____

At the end of the month, sit down and discuss what each of you has learned, and make plans to change anything about the responsibilities that seems appropriate at that time.

Remember to bring completed worksheet to your next appointment.

INTIMACY

GOALS OF THE EXERCISE

1. To help couples discover the things that enhance their feelings of closeness.
2. To help couples increase the actions that enhance intimacy.

TYPES OF PROBLEMS THIS EXERCISE MAY BE MOST USEFUL FOR

*   Communication Issues
*   Infidelity
*   Jealousy
*   Sexual Dysfunction

SUGGESTIONS FOR PROCESSING THIS EXERCISE WITH THE COUPLE

1. What things helped each of you feel closer to your partner?
2. What makes those things more likely to occur?
3. What changes do you plan to make now that you have noticed these things about the intimacy in your relationship?

INTIMACY

Intimacy is something that is hard to define, but you know when it's there. It is hard to make yourself feel more intimate, but sometimes you can do things that will make you feel closer. If you are looking to increase your intimacy, you might find it helpful to track your feelings of intimacy, see what is different when you feel closer to your partner, and then make those things happen more often.

Using the following graph, imagine your intimacy on a scale of 0 to 10, with 0 being before you knew each other and 10 being the closest you've ever felt. Each day between now and your next session, plot your feelings of intimacy from 1 to 10. Note what helped you feel closer that day or at least what helped you feel as close as you did. Use another sheet of paper if necessary.

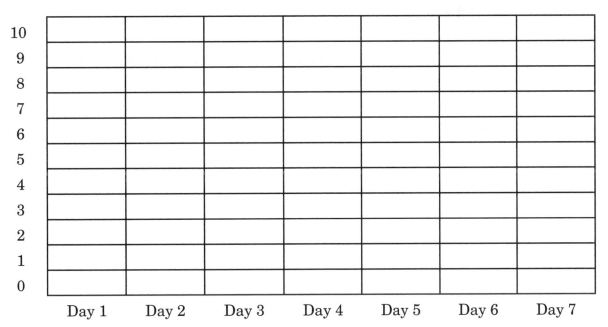

Remember to bring completed worksheet to your next appointment.

STYLES OF AND MOTIVATION FOR ARGUING

GOALS OF THE EXERCISE

1. To encourage the couple to slow down and think.
2. To suggest specific changes to help in discussing differences.

TYPES OF PROBLEMS THIS EXERCISE MAY BE MOST USEFUL FOR

- Anger
- Blame
- Communication Issues
- Personality Differences

SUGGESTIONS FOR PROCESSING THIS EXERCISE WITH THE COUPLE

1. What helped?
2. Did you come to any new understandings beyond what assignment sheet suggested?
3. What was difficult and how did you deal with it?

STYLES OF AND MOTIVATION FOR ARGUING

Just about anything can become a habit, and that includes arguing. One of the best ways to break a habit is to make it impossible to perform. You can do that by continuing what you do, but changing a detail that makes it a slightly different behavior from what you did in the past. This is an exercise in changing your style of arguing. It may give you ideas about other things you can change as well.

Between now and your next session, be alert to the subtle beginnings of an argument. At the first hint or suspicion of an impending argument, remind your partner that this is an opportunity to work on changing old habits. The person who first suspects that the argument is starting goes first. Go to separate rooms. Write whatever it is that you want to say. When finished, give the paper to your partner, who then has the opportunity to read it and respond on paper. Repeat this process as long as you think it is helpful. Then answer the following questions:

1. How did the course of the argument differ from your usual disagreements?

   _____

   _____

2. What was better about doing it this way?

   _____

   _____

3. What were the disadvantages?

   _____

   _____

4. What can you take from this experience and apply to your disagreements in the future?

   _____

   _____

Remember to bring completed worksheet to your next appointment.

FORGIVENESS

GOALS OF THE EXERCISE

1. To move clients closer to forgiveness about something about which they have been holding feelings of resentment and a desire for vengeance.
2. To help clients recognize the price they pay for anger and resentment.
3. To challenge the client to either get satisfaction from the other person or let go of the urge to get even.

TYPES OF PROBLEMS THIS EXERCISE MAY BE MOST USEFUL FOR

- Anger
- Communication Issues
- Infidelity
- Jealousy
- Physical Abuse
- Sexual Abuse

SUGGESTIONS FOR PROCESSING THIS EXERCISE WITH THE COUPLE

1. What do you feel you are owed?
2. What are the advantages and disadvantages of remaining angry?
3. Have you let the other person know what you want?
4. How will you know that you have forgiven the other person?

FORGIVENESS

While it is common for people to hold a grudge when they have been wronged, there is a growing body of evidence that suggests that unresolved anger is bad for your physical and mental health. While it may be impossible and even undesirable to forget what happened, it is surprising what some people can forgive. What is forgiveness? A popular definition holds that when you forgive, you simply write off any debt that you feel is owed to you. In other words, it is a decision.

1. What do you think would even the score?

    _____

    _____

    _____

2. What price do you pay for holding on to this debt?

    _____

    _____

    _____

3. Have you let the other person know what you think you are owed?

    _____

    _____

    _____

4. If not, would you?

    _____

    _____

    _____

5. Can they or are they willing to give you what you want?

    _____

    _____

    _____

6. How would you be better off if you gave up on getting even?

    _____

    _____

    _____

7. How long are you willing to hold on to your anger?

    _____

    _____

    _____

Get perspective:

Sometimes the things we hold on to and focus on can be placed in context when we see the things others have forgiven and lived with. Find a story or example that reframes your grudge. There are many Web sites, articles, books, and other potential sources.

Remember to bring completed worksheet to your next appointment.

MONEY/FINANCIAL CONFLICTS

GOALS OF THE EXERCISE

1. To help the couple get a clear idea of how their money is used.
2. To encourage the couple to make conscious decisions after discussion about where to spend their money.

TYPES OF PROBLEMS THIS EXERCISE MAY BE MOST USEFUL FOR

*   Financial Conflict
*   Job Stress
*   Work/Home Role Strain

SUGGESTIONS FOR PROCESSING THIS EXERCISE WITH THE COUPLE

1. In what categories did you spend the most money?
2. In what categories did you spend the least money?
3. What surprised you?
4. What do you like about how you spent your money?
5. How do you want to change?
6. What will be difficult about changing?

MONEY/FINANCIAL CONFLICTS

Money serves a wide variety of purposes for people. If you are going to control your finances, it will help to know where your money goes and what need it is filling for you. There is an old saying: "If you don't know where you are, it's hard to get to where you want to go." This exercise is a good way to find out where you are in regard to money and to begin thinking about your relationship and priorities with money.

Keep track of where you spend every penny for one month (especially cash). You may need to carry a little notebook with you at all times to record the data. Enter the totals here, adding as many additional categories as you need. Avoid creating a miscellaneous category; be specific.

ATM fees

Auto/gas

Cable

Charity

Childcare

Cleaning supplies

Clothing

Computer/software

Credit card interest

Dental

Diapers

Eating out

Entertainment

Gifts

Groceries

Hobbies

Home improvement

Housing

Insurance

Liquor

Medical

Savings

School expenses

Telephone

Tobacco

Toiletries

Transportation

Utilities

As you look over the totals, what surprises you?

_____

_____

During this month, how much did you save?

_____

_____

What would you like to change?

_____

_____

_____

_____

What steps are you willing to take toward those changes?

_____

_____

_____

Remember to bring completed worksheet to your next appointment.

A COMMON DESTINATION

GOALS OF THE EXERCISE

1. To help the couple get a clear idea of their vacation preferences.
2. To help the couple find and plan a mutually agreeable vacation.
3. To help the couple develop new problem-solving skills.

TYPES OF PROBLEMS THIS EXERCISE MAY BE MOST USEFUL FOR

- Communication Issues
- Recreational Activities Dispute

SUGGESTIONS FOR PROCESSING THIS EXERCISE WITH THE COUPLE

1. In what categories did you agree the most?
2. Did you clarify anything for yourself about your vacation preferences?
3. What surprised you about your partner's lists?
4. Based on this exercise, could you now make a mutually agreeable vacation plan for your next vacation?
5. If not, could you agree to let each partner plan every other vacation, taking into account the other partner's preferences?

A COMMON DESTINATION

Vacations are supposed to be times of rest and relaxation; however, sometimes couples disagree on their preferred styles of vacation or destination. This exercise may help resolve conflicts about vacations.

1. Each of you should describe your ideal vacation, including ideal locations, ideal activities during a vacation, and friends you wouldn't mind having along or would like to have along with you:

    _____

    _____

    _____

    _____

    _____

    _____

    Ideal length of vacation:

    _____

    Ideal frequency of vacation:

    _____

    Ideal time of the year for vacation:

    _____

    Ideal amount of money or limit for expenditures for vacation:

    _____

2. Compare notes with your partner. Don't judge or make fun of your partner's preferences. List on a separate sheet any common areas of agreement on your lists.

3. Find three vacations that fulfill as many of your common preferences as possible and write them here.

    _____

    _____

    _____

Remember to bring completed worksheet to your next appointment.

NEGOTIATING SOCIALIZING PREFERENCE DIFFERENCES

GOALS OF THE EXERCISE

1. To help the couple get a clear idea of their socializing preferences.
2. To help the couple find and plan mutually agreeable social arrangements.

TYPES OF PROBLEMS THIS EXERCISE MAY BE MOST USEFUL FOR

- Blended-Family Problems
- Communication Issues
- Job Stress
- Recreational Activities Dispute
- Work/Home Role Strain

SUGGESTIONS FOR PROCESSING THIS EXERCISE WITH THE COUPLE

1. In what categories did you agree the most?
2. Did you clarify anything for yourself about your preferences?
3. What surprised you about your partner's lists?
4. Based on this exercise, could you now make mutually agreeable social plans?

NEGOTIATING SOCIALIZING PREFERENCE DIFFERENCES

Sometimes couples disagree about how they want to spend their social time or how much they want to interact with each other or others outside of their relationship. At one time, the big complaint was spending time with the in-laws. Now, dual careers, the Internet, computer games, and the proliferation of television channels and videos provide many areas of potential conflict and distraction. This exercise may help clarify and resolve conflicts about these areas.

1. Each of you should make a list of how you like to spend your social time.

   Individual time

   How much? _____

   Doing what? _____

   Time with your partner

   How much? _____

   Doing what? _____

   Time with friends

   How much? _____

   Doing what? _____

   Time with children

   How much? _____

   Doing what? _____

   Time with other family members

   How much? _____

   Doing what? _____

   Time with in-laws

   How much? _____

   Doing what? _____

Time with extended family

How much? _____

Doing what? _____

Hobbies

How much? _____

Doing what? _____

Together or alone? _____

Entertainment

How much? _____

Doing what? _____

Together or alone? _____

2. Compare notes with your partner. Don't judge or make fun of your partner's preferences. List on a separate sheet any common areas of agreement on your list.

3. Negotiate, perhaps with the help of your counselor, areas of disagreement.

    Remember to bring completed worksheet to your next appointment.

CREATING A MISSION

GOALS OF THE EXERCISE

1. To define a common purpose.
2. To provide a reminder of purpose.

TYPES OF PROBLEMS THIS EXERCISE MAY BE MOST USEFUL FOR

- Empty Nesters
- Infidelity
- Premarriage

SUGGESTIONS FOR PROCESSING THIS EXERCISE WITH THE COUPLE

1. How might you use your mission statement to help you set goals and make decisions?
2. Where will you keep your mission statement so you are reminded of it frequently?
3. How would you know if you got sidetracked from your mission?
4. What sort of ritual might you establish to help you remain on your mission?

CREATING A MISSION

Listed here are some things and activities people value. If the things important to you are not on the list, feel free to add them. Now go through the list and indicate the importance you place on each item.

1. It's essential.
2. It's desired.
3. Take it or leave it.
4. I'm against it.

Do this now.

_____ Daily alone time	_____ Housekeeping
_____ Spending time with personal friends	_____ Driving a late model automobile
_____ Spending time with other couples	_____ Sending children to private school
_____ Personal hobbies	_____ Sending children to college
_____ Disciplining the children	_____ Praying together at home
_____ Helping children with homework	_____ Taking a family vacation
_____ Spending one-on-one time with children	_____ Taking a couple-only vacation
_____ Family activities	_____ Taking a vacation alone
_____ Attending church regularly	_____ Regular date night
_____ Cooking and eating at home	_____ Saving for retirement
_____ Family dinner	_____ Saving for emergencies
_____ Facilitating children's out-of-school activities	_____ Providing health insurance
_____ Spending time with your family of origin	_____ Being active in civic groups

_____ Spending time with in-laws   _____ Personal health and fitness

_____ Owning a house   _____ Spouse's health and fitness

_____ Home improvement/lawn care   _____ Children's health and fitness

_____ _____   _____ _____

_____ _____   _____ _____

_____ _____   _____ _____

What conclusions can you draw from your choices?

_____

_____

_____

_____

What difficulties can you anticipate?

_____

_____

_____

_____

Compare your thoughts with your partner's.

Write a paragraph that generally expresses the values you both hold and the type of household you hope to create. Don't worry about details. Try for a general statement of purpose.

_____

_____

_____

_____

_____

_____

_____

_____

Example of a brief mission statement:

Our mission is to provide a loving, supportive, and safe atmosphere in which we and our children can grow and explore the things we find meaningful. We acknowledge that this will require balancing our individual needs and desires with what is best for our family as a whole. We endeavor to maintain this balance through openness and honesty.

Remember to bring completed worksheet to your next appointment.

CHRONIC OR UNPRODUCTIVE ARGUMENTS

GOALS OF THE EXERCISE

1. To help couples interrupt and change unproductive conflict patterns and habits.
2. To help both partners find new ways of accomplishing their goals more effectively.

TYPES OF PROBLEMS THIS EXERCISE MAY BE MOST USEFUL FOR

- Anger
- Blame
- Communication Issues
- Intolerance

SUGGESTIONS FOR PROCESSING THIS EXERCISE WITH THE COUPLE

1. Was there anything on the tape that surprised you?
2. Was there anything that embarrassed you?
3. What do you plan to change based on this exercise?

CHRONIC OR UNPRODUCTIVE ARGUMENTS

Some arguments seem to get repeated over and over with nothing getting settled. Sometimes this happens because we are so involved in the argument that we don't stop to listen to ourselves. This assignment is designed to help you do that and to see what a difference that can make.

Tape-record one of your arguments. Do this only with the full knowledge and consent of both persons. Later, find a calm time to review the argument. Before you listen to the tape, write as clearly as possible what you were trying to accomplish. In this step, be careful to define what you were trying to resolve (for example, "Deciding how to manage our money in a responsible way") and not the solution you were suggesting (for example, "Getting him or her to stop spending so much money on clothes").

_____
_____
_____
_____
_____

Now review the tape, stopping it every three minutes (or more often if appropriate). Note everything that either of you does that moves you even a little bit toward your goal as you have stated it. For the purposes of this exercise, do your best to ignore the things that don't move the two of you toward your goal.

_____
_____
_____
_____

When you are finished:

What did you learn from this exercise?

_____
_____
_____

Would it help to do it again? Why or why not?

_____

_____

_____

_____

How can you use this information in future discussions?

_____

_____

_____

_____

Remember to bring completed worksheet to your next appointment.

VERBAL ABUSE

GOALS OF THE EXERCISE

1. To help couples recognize and identify verbal abuse.
2. To help the partner who feels verbally abused escape from some of the damage to his or her confidence or self-esteem.

TYPES OF PROBLEMS THIS EXERCISE MAY BE MOST USEFUL FOR

- Anger
- Blame
- Communication Issues
- Psychological Abuse

SUGGESTIONS FOR PROCESSING THIS EXERCISE WITH THE COUPLE

1. Did this exercise help either of you make any changes?
2. Did it help you recognize or learn anything new?
3. What kinds of things did you write on your lists?

VERBAL ABUSE

Verbal abuse is an attempt to control or manipulate someone by using words or speaking in a manner that demeans them. If you live with a person who verbally abuses you, it can be very difficult to keep a realistic image of yourself. Here are some suggestions that may help.

By identifying verbal abuse, you can remind yourself that you needn't accept it. Remember that verbal abuse is about control and manipulation. Write out some of the abusive words or expressions that your partner uses.

_____

_____

_____

_____

List names and phone numbers of people you know and trust to have objective opinions of you.

_____

_____

_____

_____

Look up and write down the phone number(s) of your local abuse prevention service(s). Use them if you need them.

_____

_____

_____

_____

Write three messages of self-affirmation or encouragement that you know to be true about yourself but sometimes forget after you've been attacked.

_____

_____

_____

List any inspirational books, pictures, mementos, or other items that you can look at and touch when you need to remind yourself of your self-worth.

_____

_____

_____

_____

Write your reason(s) for staying in this abusive situation and review them from time to time to see if they still make sense to you.

_____

_____

_____

_____

Keep this paper in a safe place so you can find it when you need support.

_____

_____

_____

_____

Remember to bring completed worksheet to your next appointment.

BOXING CLUTTER TO A TKO

GOALS OF THE EXERCISE

1. To help couples find a resolution to conflicts about clutter and procrastination.
2. To help the procrastinating partner get moving to clean up the clutter.
3. To empower the other partner.

TYPES OF PROBLEMS THIS EXERCISE MAY BE MOST USEFUL FOR

- Life-Changing Events
- Work/Home Role Strain

SUGGESTIONS FOR PROCESSING THIS EXERCISE WITH THE COUPLE

1. How did it feel to put the date or have the date put on the box?
2. Does this exercise feel as if it will be helpful in resolving your conflicts about clutter and procrastination?
3. What do you fear will happen in a year? What do you hope will happen in a year?

BOXING CLUTTER TO A TKO

If one of you keeps old mail, papers, articles, magazines, and other things that clutter the house but could be gone through, organized, and thrown out or filed, and it drives the other partner crazy, you might try this idea.

The partner who is most bothered by the clutter can gather up the mess and place it into a box. The box is then labeled with a date one year from the day the clutter is placed in the box. The box can be stored in a closet or garage or left out in the open. By the date on the box, the other partner must have gone through, organized, and cleaned out the box, or the other partner has permission to throw the box out.

Use the rest of this page to make notes about anything you want to remember to discuss with your therapist in your next session.

_____
_____
_____
_____
_____
_____
_____
_____
_____
_____

Remember to bring completed worksheet to your next appointment.

SEPARATING WORK FROM HOME LIFE

GOALS OF THE EXERCISE

1. To help the couple clarify areas in which work impinges on home life in an unhelpful way.
2. To help the couple make changes to separate home from work.

TYPES OF PROBLEMS THIS EXERCISE MAY BE MOST USEFUL FOR

*   Anger
*   Depression Independent of Relationship Problems
*   Financial Conflict
*   Job Stress
*   Work/Home Role Strain

SUGGESTIONS FOR PROCESSING THIS EXERCISE WITH THE COUPLE

1. Which areas are the most crucial in making the separation of work from home life?
2. In which areas did you both agree that work is impinging unhelpfully on home life?
3. What was the agreement you made?

SEPARATING WORK FROM HOME LIFE

If you have a conflict around separating your home life from your work life or your partner's, use this exercise to clarify and negotiate a good separation of one area from the other.

1. List the ways that one or both of you think that work life impinges on your home life, your relationship, or your family life and time. Examine these areas:

    *   Working late
    *   Computer use
    *   Time at work versus time at home, with family, friends, or spouse
    *   Space (work taking over areas at home)
    *   People (work relationships impinging on home)
    *   Phone calls (at home from work or from home to work)

2. Have a discussion about changes that either or both of you would like in any of these areas.

    _____

    _____

    _____

3. Make an agreement for either or both of you to make at least three changes over the next six months.

    _____

    _____

    _____

Remember to bring completed worksheet to your next appointment.

PLANNED SPONTANEITY

GOALS OF THE EXERCISE

1. To revitalize the couple's romantic life.
2. To help people learn how to be more romantic from their past, from books, and from others.

TYPES OF PROBLEMS THIS EXERCISE MAY BE MOST USEFUL FOR

*   Anxiety
*   Depression Due to Relationship Problems
*   Infidelity
*   Jealousy
*   Loss of Love/Affection
*   Sexual Dysfunction

SUGGESTIONS FOR PROCESSING THIS EXERCISE WITH THE COUPLE

1. Did you feel more loving as you did more romantic things?
2. Did your partner seem more loving to you after you did some more romantic things?
3. How could you use what you learned from doing this exercise in your future relationship?

PLANNED SPONTANEITY

It takes ongoing effort to keep a relationship fresh and alive. But what if you're among the ranks of the romantically challenged? For many people, exciting, spontaneous activities are things they observe others doing that make them say, "Why don't I think of doing those things?" One way to answer this query is to plan some spontaneous activities that break your old mold. Remember that many new activities feel awkward and uncomfortable when you are learning them. If you do this exercise frequently enough, you may find that you start to enjoy being romantic.

1. List 10 or more things that you and your partner have done that he or she considered romantic.

   _____

   _____

   _____

   _____

   _____

   _____

   _____

   _____

   _____

   _____

   _____

   _____

   _____

   _____

   _____

   _____

   _____

   _____

2. Go to the library or bookstore and find one of the many popular books that give ideas for romantic things to do. Find 10 or more romantic things that you would consider doing, and write them here.

_____

_____

_____

_____

_____

_____

_____

_____

_____

_____

3. Over the next month, watch and listen to what goes on around you for things that other people do that are signs of caring. Listen to coworkers. Pay attention to television shows. Use any and all sources of information. Note five things you learn.

_____

_____

_____

_____

_____

4. Once a week, get out your list and look it over for inspiration. Plan a specific time to surprise your partner with your activity.

Feel free to add to your list in the future and indicate things that are particularly successful.

Remember to bring completed worksheet to your next appointment.

A SAFE PLACE FOR THE TRAUMATIC MEMORIES

GOALS OF THE EXERCISE

1. To safely contain the trauma of the affair.
2. To get the details of the affair acknowledged in a way that doesn't create so much post-traumatic stress.

TYPES OF PROBLEMS THIS EXERCISE MAY BE MOST USEFUL FOR

*   Infidelity
*   Jealousy
*   Life-Changing Event

SUGGESTIONS FOR PROCESSING THIS EXERCISE WITH THE COUPLE

1. How was it to write or record the details of the affair?
2. How is it to know that those details have been acknowledged?
3. Is it better to have those details locked up for a while?

A SAFE PLACE FOR THE TRAUMATIC MEMORIES

Sometimes the person who has been betrayed is obsessed with learning details about the affair. These details can become an obsession that prevents the person who has been betrayed from letting go of the hurt.

Don't ask your partner for details. You may hear things that will haunt you for years, images that you will find hard to forget or get over. Once you know the broad outlines of what happened, let it rest for a while. If you find you are still haunted by questions, have your partner write out or record all the details and put the record of the affair in a safe-deposit box. Give the key to a friend with instructions not to let you have the key for a year. If you still feel the need to know, look at the material after a year. Most people don't want to see it by then, as they have some distance and don't want to reopen themselves to the pain.

CHRONIC LATENESS FROM WORK

GOALS OF THE EXERCISE

1. To help the couple interrupt and change unproductive conflicts about lateness when returning home from work.
2. To create an incentive for the late partner to come home on time.

TYPES OF PROBLEMS THIS EXERCISE MAY BE MOST USEFUL FOR

*   Financial Conflict
*   Jealousy
*   Job Stress
*   Work/Home Role Strain

SUGGESTIONS FOR PROCESSING THIS EXERCISE WITH THE COUPLE

1. What changed as a result of this exercise?
2. Did the late partner come home any earlier?
3. What kinds of effort did it take to get home on time?
4. Did you get more time to do what you wanted as a couple, and was it worth it?

CHRONIC LATENESS FROM WORK

If you are constantly arguing about one partner coming home late from work, try this exercise. Stop hassling the partner who is late. Stop complaining ineffectively. Agree on a time that both of you think is reasonable and gives the person who is late some leeway. For every minute the partner is late, the other partner gets to redeem a minute at the end of the week for doing anything as a couple that he or she would like to do.

Write the target time here: _____

Record the following information:

Day 1

Time arrived: _____

Target time: _____

Difference, if actual time is later than target time: _____

If you arrived on time, how did you make that happen? _____

_____

Day 2

Time arrived: _____

Target time: _____

Difference, if actual time is later than target time: _____

If you arrived on time, how did you make that happen? _____

_____

Day 3

Time arrived: _____

Target time: _____

Difference, if actual time is later than target time: _____

If you arrived on time, how did you make that happen? _____

_____

Day 4

Time arrived: _____

Target time: _____

Difference, if actual time is later than target time: _____

If you arrived on time, how did you make that happen? _____

_____

Day 5

Time arrived: _____

Target time: _____

Difference, if actual time is later than target time: _____

If you arrived on time, how did you make that happen? _____

_____

Day 6

Time arrived: _____

Target time: _____

Difference, if actual time is later than target time: _____

If you arrived on time, how did you make that happen? _____

_____

Remember to bring completed worksheet to your next appointment.

SET LIMITS WITH CONSEQUENCES

GOALS OF THE EXERCISE

1. To help one partner draw limits for safety.
2. To help stop violence or dangerous behavior in the relationship.

TYPES OF PROBLEMS THIS EXERCISE MAY BE MOST USEFUL FOR

- Alcohol Abuse
- Anger
- Eating Disorder
- Infidelity
- Jealousy
- Physical Abuse

SUGGESTIONS FOR PROCESSING THIS EXERCISE WITH THE COUPLE

1. Are you ready to have the conversation?
2. Tell me your plan and the words you will use.
3. What will you do if your partner won't cooperate or gets belligerent?

SET LIMITS WITH CONSEQUENCES

Sometimes even though you've used all your communication skills, your partner may continue to act abusively or otherwise cause harm to you or someone else. When you reach that realization, you may want to draw the line. You may know that you've reached this point when you are more concerned with protecting yourself or someone else than in changing your partner's behavior. This exercise can help you clarify your thinking in an emotional situation.

State the behavior that you can no longer tolerate.

_____

_____

_____

What are the limits of what you are willing to tolerate? Be as specific as possible.

_____

_____

_____

What consequences are you willing to set if the limits are crossed? Be absolutely certain that the consequence is something under your control and that you are willing to act on it.

_____

_____

_____

How can you present this to your partner so that it is most likely to be taken seriously and to be seen not so much as an ultimatum as something you are doing to take care of personal needs that you deserve to have met.

_____

_____

_____

Where and when will you have your conversation?

_____
_____
_____

What words will you use? A statement of what you will do is suggested over a statement of what your partner must do.

_____
_____
_____

Do you need to take any measures for your safety?

_____
_____
_____

Remember to bring completed worksheet to your next appointment.

MIX 'N' MATCH SEXUAL MENU FOR EXPANDING YOUR SEX LIFE

GOALS OF THE EXERCISE

1. To help couples communicate their sexual interests to each other.
2. To help couples revitalize their sexual relationship.

TYPES OF PROBLEMS THIS EXERCISE MAY BE MOST USEFUL FOR

- Communication Issues
- Jealousy
- Loss of Love/Affection
- Sexual Dysfunction

SUGGESTIONS FOR PROCESSING THIS EXERCISE WITH THE COUPLE

1. Did doing this exercise result in any changes in your sex life?
2. What surprised you most about your own preferences? Your partner's?
3. Do you think this is a helpful exercise for you as a couple and that you would do it again sometime in the future?

MIX 'N' MATCH SEXUAL MENU FOR EXPANDING YOUR SEX LIFE

Many couples grow stale in their sexual life, in part because they fall into routines and in part because they don't tell each other new sexual things they might like to try. Others find that their preferences change, and if they never talk about it, they don't get satisfied and lose interest. This exercise can help restore new creativity and excitement to your sex life.

The two columns that follow represent the parts of our bodies that are capable of providing stimulation to others (the doers) and those parts of our bodies that are capable of experiencing stimulation or pleasure (the doees). Add your own body parts to the list if there are any missing. Your task is to draw a line between each of these columns to indicate which might be interesting for you to explore or are activities that you really enjoy. After you connect the columns with lines, discuss your choices with your partner. You may want to do the chart together, but if you do it alone, show your chart to your partner and talk about it. You may want to exchange lists and keep them for future reference.

The Doers	The Doees
Fingers	Mouth
Tongue	Penis
Penis	Vagina
Vagina	Breasts
Mouth	Nipples
Hand	Anus
Skin	Clitoris
	Skin

Feel free to add in the remaining space anything that you would like your partner to know about what gives you pleasure.

_____

_____

Remember to bring completed worksheet to your next appointment.

PLEASURE TEACHING SESSION

GOALS OF THE EXERCISE

1. To facilitate couples learning about each other's sexual preferences.
2. To revitalize the couple's sexual life.

TYPES OF PROBLEMS THIS EXERCISE MAY BE MOST USEFUL FOR

- Communication Issues
- Jealousy
- Loss of Love/Affection
- Sexual Dysfunction

SUGGESTIONS FOR PROCESSING THIS EXERCISE WITH THE COUPLE

1. Which role was easier for you? What does this say about you?
2. What was most difficult about this exercise for you?
3. What were three things you learned?
4. What does it say about you as a couple that you carried out this assignment?

PLEASURE TEACHING SESSION

Pick a time when you both have nothing pressing or scheduled. Reserve several hours and find a private place. You may have to rent a hotel room if you have children at home. Choose which person is to be the teacher and which is the student. The student's task is to learn from the teacher what gives the teacher pleasure. The teacher may use words, sounds, pictures, or guided movements to indicate what feels good (and, of course, what doesn't feel good). The teacher must be sure to bring whatever materials are necessary to enhance his or her pleasure (special clothes or outfits, sexual toys, massage oil, condoms, books, videotapes, etc.). The student may also bring items he or she thinks would bring pleasure, but may only introduce them with the teacher's permission. On another occasion, switch roles, with the student becoming the teacher.

DEALING WITH IMPOTENCE

GOALS OF THE EXERCISE

1. To facilitate couples working together to resolve impotence.
2. To take the pressure off the male to perform sexually.

TYPES OF PROBLEMS THIS EXERCISE MAY BE MOST USEFUL FOR

- Communication Issues
- Jealousy
- Life-Changing Events
- Loss of Love/Affection
- Sexual Dysfunction

SUGGESTIONS FOR PROCESSING THIS EXERCISE WITH THE COUPLE

1. What did you learn from this exercise?
2. Did the man have a stronger and longer-lasting erection doing this exercise?
3. What did you talk about during the discussion part of the exercise?

DEALING WITH IMPOTENCE

Part of the problem with impotence is the pressure men put on themselves to perform. This exercise is designed to remove much of that pressure. Barring physical causes or medication, many times sexual arousal returns if you just relax and enjoy the process rather than trying to force a response.

1. Create a safe time and place where you can talk over the experience of impotence. How do you each feel about it? Don't be so careful or nice that you don't express all that you need to say.

2. Have the male partner tell the other partner what internal thoughts and actions add to the feeling of pressure to perform.

3. Arrange at least three times in which you as a couple have a sexual experience in which erections do not play a part.

HELP FOR PREMATURE EJACULATION

GOALS OF THE EXERCISE

1. To facilitate couples working together to resolve premature ejaculation.
2. To help the make partner learn to delay ejaculation.

TYPES OF PROBLEMS THIS EXERCISE MAY BE MOST USEFUL FOR

- Communication Issues
- Dependency
- Jealousy
- Loss of Love/Affection
- Sexual Dysfunction

SUGGESTIONS FOR PROCESSING THIS EXERCISE WITH THE COUPLE

1. What did you learn from this exercise?
2. Did the man have a stronger and longer-lasting erection doing this exercise?
3. Which method worked best for you?

HELP FOR PREMATURE EJACULATION

The first thing to say about premature ejaculation is that many men ejaculate fairly quickly during intercourse. For some couples this becomes a problem and for others it never becomes an issue. Part of what makes it an issue for some couples is that the partner does not have a chance to have an orgasm through intercourse. This can be helped by ensuring that the other partner is either sufficiently aroused to reach a climax quickly or has had an orgasm before intercourse through oral or manual stimulation. Here are two other experiments to try that may help.

1.   The man must learn to attend to the sensations of an approaching orgasm and then slow down and stop moving before he gets to the point of no return. Many men feel they have to perform or keep moving to give their partners pleasure. Delaying ejaculation is a skill that can be learned. Work together to help the male partner learn to slow down and enjoy the process. Make an agreement before you have intercourse that the other partner will say when the male partner must stop moving. Try this one time in the next week.

2.   The man can masturbate to ejaculation an hour or so before intercourse. This often decreases the man's sensitivity or delays future ejaculations. Try this one time during the next week and find out whether it helps and is satisfying for both partners.

INITIATION WEEK

GOAL OF THE EXERCISE

1. To change the couple's sexual initiation patterns.

TYPES OF PROBLEMS THIS EXERCISE MAY BE MOST USEFUL FOR

- Communication Issues
- Jealousy
- Loss of Love/Affection
- Midlife Crisis
- Sexual Dysfunction

SUGGESTIONS FOR PROCESSING THIS EXERCISE WITH THE COUPLE

1. What did you learn from this exercise?
2. How did this challenge your ideas about yourself and your partner sexually?
3. Were you uncomfortable about initiating or having your partner initiate?

INITIATION WEEK

Most couples get into patterns and habits in which one partner initiates sex. How about trying something new?

1. The partner who usually doesn't initiate sex agrees to initiate one time in the next week, with the condition that it not be at bedtime.

2. After sex, spend at least 10 minutes discussing both or your experiences with this switched initiation of sex.

3. For the partner who initiated:
   - What was the most difficult thing about this for you?

   _____

   _____

   - How did you decide when to make your move?

   _____

   _____

   - What did you learn?

   _____

   _____

4. For the other:
   - Was this more like what you've been wanting?

   _____

   _____

   - What did you like about the way your partner initiated sex?

   _____

   _____

   - Were there any disadvantages to being in your position?

   _____

   _____

5. Would it help to do this exercise again?

   _____

   _____

Remember to bring completed worksheet to your next appointment.

LIGHTENING UP ABOUT SEXUALITY AND WEIGHT GAIN

GOALS OF THE EXERCISE

1. To get the couple's focus off weight and onto sexual actions that they can change more easily.
2. To restore or enhance the couple's sexual life.

TYPES OF PROBLEMS THIS EXERCISE MAY BE MOST USEFUL FOR

- Communication Issues
- Jealousy
- Loss of Love/Affection
- Midlife Crisis
- Sexual Dysfunction

SUGGESTIONS FOR PROCESSING THIS EXERCISE WITH THE COUPLE

1. Did you find that this exercise enhanced or restored any of your sexual life?
2. Did you find this exercise helpful in other ways?
3. How can you use this or similar ideas in the future or in other areas of your relationship?

LIGHTENING UP ABOUT SEXUALITY
AND WEIGHT GAIN

When one partner tells the other that they are no longer sexually attracted to them because they have gained too much weight, there are ways of making some changes.

Focusing on the weight issue is unproductive. Usually your partner is self-conscious or unhappy about his or her weight. Focusing on it only leads to more self-consciousness and unhappiness. Instead, focus on things that either one of you could do sexually. Doing some sexual or sensual things together often restores excitement to your sex life.

Tell your partner three things that you would like to do sexually with him or her that would be exciting. These can be either things you have done before or new things you would like to try. Remember that many parts of the body can be sensual and that the most important sex organ is between your ears. You can each list three or more things here:

_____

_____

_____

_____

_____

_____

Discuss these things and find at least one of them that both of you are willing to try.

Make a commitment to trying this sexual experiment within the next week.

Remember to bring completed worksheet to your next appointment.

A NIGHT TO REMEMBER

GOALS OF THE EXERCISE

1. To get the couple to reclaim the elements of their best remembered sexual experience.
2. To restore or enhance the couple's sexual life.

TYPES OF PROBLEMS THIS EXERCISE MAY BE MOST USEFUL FOR

- Communication Issues
- Jealousy
- Loss of Love/Affection
- Midlife Crisis
- Sexual Dysfunction

SUGGESTIONS FOR PROCESSING THIS EXERCISE WITH THE COUPLE

1. Did you find that this exercise enhanced or restored any of your sexual life?
2. Did you find this exercise helpful in other ways?
3. How can you use this or similar ideas in the future or in other areas of your relationship?

A NIGHT TO REMEMBER

Many couples think wistfully about the good old days when their sex was passionate and plentiful. You may feel as if those days are gone forever or that you have to resort to more and more wild and radical activities to get as turned on as you used to. But it may be simpler than that.

In this exercise, you are going to be the archeologists of your passion, uncovering previous experiences that you might dust off and reclaim for use in the present and the future.

Think of the best sexual experience you have had together as a couple.

Each of you should make your own list. List three things in each of these areas that helped make that sex good.

What you did:

1. _____

2. _____

3. _____

What your partner did:

1. _____

2. _____

3. _____

What environment were you in:

1. _____

2. _____

3. _____

What happened before, during, and after:

1. _____

2. _____

3. _____

Discuss these things and find at least one of them that both of you are willing to try.

Make a commitment to trying this sexual experiment within the next week.

Remember to bring completed worksheet to your next appointment.

WRESTLING WITH THE CHALLENGING TASK OF PARENTING

GOALS OF THE EXERCISE

1. To normalize the experience of being overwhelmed by parenting at times.
2. To give the couple practice at taking breaks from parenting in a cooperative way.

TYPES OF PROBLEMS THIS EXERCISE MAY BE MOST USEFUL FOR

- Blended-Family Problems
- Communication Issues
- Parenting Conflicts—Adolescents
- Parenting Conflicts—Children

SUGGESTIONS FOR PROCESSING THIS EXERCISE WITH THE COUPLE

1. What did you learn from this exercise?
2. What other ideas did you get about supporting each other as parents?
3. How did your children react?

WRESTLING WITH THE CHALLENGING TASK OF PARENTING

Everybody has their limits, and kids sometimes can take you there and beyond. Before that happens, take a tip from the world of professional wrestling. Wait! Don't put a full nelson on them. Use the tag-team approach and let your partner take over for a while.

You may have seen tag-team wrestling. One member of the team is allowed in the ring at a time (at least those are the rules). When that member gets into a tight spot, he or she is able to tag a team member outside the ring and that person takes over.

Discuss this concept with your partner and plan in advance how you will let your partner know you need to switch. You might want to discuss the advantages of waiting until the tag takes place before your partner enters the ring.

List five ways you will know it is time to get help.

_____
_____
_____
_____
_____

Track the times you make a switch.

Date: _____

What was happening: _____
How did you know it was time to switch?

_____
_____
_____

How did this make a difference?

_____
_____
_____

Date: _____

What was happening: _____

How did you know it was time to switch?

_____

_____

_____

How did this make a difference?

_____

_____

_____

Date: _____

What was happening: _____

How did you know it was time to switch?

_____

_____

_____

How did this make a difference?

_____

_____

_____

Date: _____

What was happening: _____

How did you know it was time to switch?

_____

_____

_____

How did this make a difference?

_____

_____

_____

Remember to bring completed worksheet to your next appointment.

IN-LAW PROBLEMS

GOALS OF THE EXERCISE

1. To break unhelpful patterns of interactions between the couple and in-laws.
2. To give the couple or a partner a sense of empowerment in regard to the problem of intrusive in-laws.

TYPES OF PROBLEMS THIS EXERCISE MAY BE MOST USEFUL FOR

- Blended-Family Problems
- Communication Issues

SUGGESTIONS FOR PROCESSING THIS EXERCISE WITH THE COUPLE

1. Did you notice any changes from your in-law(s) when you tried this approach?
2. Did you have fun with this exercise?
3. What have you learned from it?

IN-LAW PROBLEMS

Helpful family members who offer unwanted advice can put a major strain on a relationship. Changing the game can sometimes get them to back off.

This exercise involves moving toward rather than running away from these would-be advisors. Start tracking the unsolicited advice you get from your relative. At the same time, start calling at frequent intervals asking advice about increasingly mundane issues. Keep notes of all your contacts:

Date: _____ Time: _____

    Advice given:

_____

_____

_____

_____

    Did you ask for it? _____

    Who initiated the contact? _____

Date: _____ Time: _____

    Advice given:

_____

_____

_____

_____

    Did you ask for it? _____

    Who initiated the contact? _____

Date: _____ Time: _____

    Advice given:

    _____

    _____

    _____

    _____

    Did you ask for it? _____

    Who initiated the contact? _____

Date: _____ Time: _____

    Advice given:

    _____

    _____

    _____

    _____

    Did you ask for it? _____

    Who initiated the contact? _____

Date: _____ Time: _____

    Advice given:

    _____

    _____

    _____

    _____

    Did you ask for it? _____

    Who initiated the contact? _____

Remember to bring completed worksheet to your next appointment.

GET A ROOMMATE

GOALS OF THE EXERCISE

1. To change unhelpful interactions between a stepparent and stepchildren.
2. To offer a helpful frame of reference for a stepparent in dealing more effectively with stepchildren.

TYPES OF PROBLEMS THIS EXERCISE MAY BE MOST USEFUL FOR

- Blended-Family Problems
- Communication Issues
- Parenting Conflicts—Adolescents
- Parenting Conflicts—Children

SUGGESTIONS FOR PROCESSING THIS EXERCISE WITH THE COUPLE

1. Was this exercise helpful to you?
2. How did you change your approach with your stepchildren?
3. How did the stepchildren respond?
4. Did you (the other partner) notice any changes in your partner (the stepparent) or your children from this exercise?

GET A ROOMMATE

Stepparents often have a difficult time defining their roles in dealing with the children of their new partner. This can be complicated further when the parent who doesn't live in the house is active in the upbringing of the children. This exercise suggests that you think of your role as "roommate." Even if you don't want to define your role this way, thinking in those terms may open some new ideas on your situation.

Think of your stepchildren as your roommates.

What are five things you expect from a roommate?

_____

_____

_____

_____

_____

What do you do when a roommate doesn't fulfill his or her responsibilities?

_____

_____

_____

_____

_____

_____

_____

_____

_____

_____

List five responsibilities you have as a roommate.

_____

_____

_____

_____

_____

How do you and your roommates keep the health department from condemning your home?

_____

_____

_____

_____

_____

Remember to bring completed worksheet to your next appointment.

CIRCLE THE WAGONS

GOALS OF THE EXERCISE

1. To strengthen the parental alliance.
2. To help the couple provide more consistent parenting.

TYPES OF PROBLEMS THIS EXERCISE MAY BE MOST USEFUL FOR

- Blended-Family Problems
- Communication Issues
- Parenting Conflicts—Adolescents
- Parenting Conflicts—Children
- Physical Abuse
- Work/Home Role Strain

SUGGESTIONS FOR PROCESSING THIS EXERCISE WITH THE COUPLE

1. How was this different from your usual ways of handling parenting conflicts or disagreements?
2. Did the children notice the difference? Did they respond any differently?
3. Were there any glitches or problems that you need to smooth out?

CIRCLE THE WAGONS

At times, being parents can put stress on any relationship, and some children seem to have a knack for homing in on the issues where parents disagree. Disagreements about consequences or rules sometimes lead to the child getting his or her own way and subverting the parental authority in a way that leaves both parents dissatisfied. Here are some ideas for handling this kind of situation.

What are five rules or consequences that you frequently disagree about?

_____

_____

_____

_____

_____

List five early signs that would let you know that a disagreement is brewing.

_____

_____

_____

_____

_____

When you notice a disagreement starting, inform the child that you are having a summit conference and retreat to a place where you can discuss the matter privately. If that is impossible at the moment, inform the child that the two of you will need to discuss the matter and you will get back to him or her.

Use the rest of the page to make notes of any conferences that you have held so you can discuss your experiences with your therapist.

_____

_____

_____

_____

_____

_____

_____

_____

_____

_____

_____

_____

_____

_____

_____

_____

_____

_____

_____

_____

_____

_____

_____

_____

_____

_____

Remember to bring completed worksheet to your next appointment.

SUGGESTIONS FOR MAKING CONVERSATIONS MORE PRODUCTIVE

- When your partner does something you don't like, stop and think before you do anything else.
- Be clear on what you want to say. Focus on what you know for sure. What are the facts, and what do you feel? Avoid assuming that you know what is going on with your partner.
- Consider presenting requests rather than making demands, unless safety issues are involved.
- When you talk, choose a good time. Make sure both of you can give your full attention and have adequate time to talk. Turn off the TV and eliminate other distractions.
- Make your motivations clear. You are not just trying to control. Your interest is in making the relationship work better.
- Hold on to your values—your relationship, for example—but be flexible on how those values get expressed.
- When you make requests, make them so clear that there is no question what you want. For instance, "try harder" or "take responsibility" are very vague. "Balance the checkbook on Saturday morning" is much clearer.
- Listen and be sure you understand before you form your reply. Take your time. This is part of a conversation you want to last a long time.
- Keep your focus on making your behavior as helpful as possible rather than on trying to control the behavior of your partner.
- If you get stuck and frustrated, call a timeout if necessary. Let the other person know that you will talk about this again, but you don't want it to get destructive. Usually 15 or 20 minutes is sufficient to calm down.
- If you are going to assume anything, assume your partner is operating in good faith and that there are reasons for his or her behaviors. If what you are hearing doesn't make sense, keep listening and asking questions.
- Try to get to the point where you both are very clear on what is needed and can commit to what you each are willing to do. Don't agree to do something you won't do.
- Consider setting a date to talk about your progress again. Write it on the calendar and make it happen.

- When you find something that works for you, try it again but also be ready to try something else.
- Add your own ideas to this process. Keep this list someplace where you can get to it when you feel you may not handle a situation in a rational way. Pick and choose the suggestions that work for you.
- Don't try to do all these at once. If you find one that looks worth trying, experiment with it until it becomes second nature.

MOVIES ABOUT COUPLES

Steffanie uses a "psycho-edu-tainment" approach to her work with clients. Books, movies, music, and other media resources can help further therapeutic goals. Couples can bring a film clip and show each other or the therapist the types of interactions that aren't working or—even better—a clip of what they would like to have happening. This can ensure that everyone is working toward the same goal. *The Story of Us* is a realistic portrayal of the process many couples go through during a marital crisis: a subtle breakdown in communication over time, a period of questioning about separation or divorce, and ultimately a resolution. *The Ref* is a black comedy that portrays a couple who sabotage and emotionally abuse each other. The interactions are so outrageous and funny that partners who would normally never acknowledge such behavior have admitted to similar dynamics. Movies can also normalize or articulate couples' reactions to various events like illness, loss, or substance abuse. *When a Man Loves a Woman* provides a quite realistic portrayal of what happens in a marriage when one partner has a substance abuse problem. *Ordinary People* is a painful but accurate representation of a family dealing with the loss of a child. Movies can also inspire and help couples persist through the challenging moments and parts of a marriage. *The Story of Us* and *When a Man Loves a Woman* provide a realistic sense of the tenuousness of negotiating relationships, yet in both films the couples are ultimately successful.

The following is a list of some movies relating to typical couples and relationship issues. The list is by no means exhaustive or complete. It is a start. We have starred some of our favorites. Add your own resources to the list.

Abuse

The Burning Bed

Affairs

Afterglow

The Age of Innocence

Alice

The Bridges of Madison County

The Brothers McMullen

Damage

Eating

Hannah and Her Sisters

Scenes from a Marriage

Something to Talk About

Terms of Endearment

Babies/Infertility

Father of the Bride Part II

For Keeps

Funny about Love

Nine Months

Parenthood

Penny Serenade

Raising Arizona

She's Having a Baby

Someone Like You

Commitment

The Age of Innocence

Beautiful Girls

The Brothers McMullen

Closer

Committed

Field of Dreams

Groundhog Day

High Fidelity

Husbands and Wives

Match Point

Nine Months

Now and Forever

Out of Africa

Shopgirl

The Story of Us

Communication

About Last Night

The Accidental Tourist

An Affair of Love

Before Sunset

Bliss

Bridget Jones's Diary
The Brothers McMullen
Committed
The Doctor
Eyes Wide Shut
The Family Man
The Four Seasons
Grand Canyon
He Said, She Said
Husbands and Wives
Lantana
Moonstruck
Mr. and Mrs. Bridge
Nine Months
The Opposite of Sex
Out of Africa
The Piano
Scenes from a Marriage
Sense and Sensibility
Shirley Valentine
The Story of Us
Tender Mercies
Two Family House
Unbreakable
Waiting to Exhale
A Walk on the Moon
What's Eating Gilbert Grape
When a Man Loves a Woman
When Harry Met Sally
You Can Count on Me

Conflict and Negotiation

The Accidental Tourist
Groundhog Day
He Said, She Said
Ordinary People
The Ref
The Story of Us

*The War of the Roses
Who's Afraid of Virginia Woolf?

Divorce
The Accidental Tourist
Bye Bye, Love
Call Me Anna
Carnal Knowledge
Damage
David's Mother
Divorce
Falling Down
The Good Mother
Husbands and Wives
Kramer vs. Kramer
Mrs. Doubtfire
Pay It Forward
The Prince of Tides
Shirley Valentine
Starting Over
Tales of Manhattan
An Unmarried Woman
The War of the Roses
The Way We Were

Illness
AIDS
Absolutely Positive
An Early Frost
Love! Valor! Compassion!
*Philadelphia
Alzheimer's/Parkinson's/Dementia
Aurora Borealis
*Away from Her
*Iris: A Memoir of Iris Murdoch
The Notebook
On Golden Pond
A Song for Martin

Asberger's/Autism
Benny and Joon
The Squid and the Whale
Blindness
80 Steps to Jonah
Ray
23 Paces to Baker Street
Deafness
Adada
Disabilities
Mask
The Miracle Worker
Passion Fish
*The Waterdance
Mental Illness
A Beautiful Mind
*Ordinary People
Severe Illness
The American Friend
Angel on My Shoulder
Bang the Drum Slowly
Lorenzo's Oil
Steel Magnolias
Terms of Endearment
Whose Life Is It Anyway?
*Wit
Traumatic Brain Injury
Regarding Henry

In-Laws
*The Birdcage
The In-Laws
The In-Laws 2
Love Crazy
Meet the Parents
Meet the Parents 2

Monsoon Wedding

The Son-in-Law

Newlyweds

Apartment for Peggy

Barefoot in the Park

The Cowboy and the Lady

Fools Rush In

The Quiet Man

She's Having a Baby

Shrek 2

You, Me and Dupree

Nontraditional Partnerships

*The Birdcage

Brokeback Mountain

Love! Valor! Compassion!

My Summer of Love

*Philadelphia

Torch Song Trilogy

Renewed Intimacy

The Accidental Tourist

Enchanted April

The Four Seasons

Pleasantville

The Story of Us

Tender Mercies

Sex and Sexuality

The Big Chill

The Color Purple

Damage

Extremities

The Four Seasons

The Good Mother

Guess Who's Coming to Dinner

He Said, She Said

Jungle Fever

Kinsey

Lady Sings the Blues

The Morning After

The Prince of Tides

Rape and Marriage

Torch Song Trilogy

The Women of Brewster Place

Substance Abuse

Candy (Australian film)

Clean and Sober

Days of Wine and Roses

I'm Dancing as Fast as I Can

Ironweed

The Lost Weekend

My Name Is Bill W.

When a Man Loves a Woman

Widowhood

Ghost

Message in a Bottle

Places in the Heart

Shadowlands

Strangers in Good Company

Truly, Madly, Deeply

AN APPRECIATIVE INTERVIEW TO CELEBRATE THE ANNIVERSARY OF YOUR MARRIAGE

CAROL ANNE KOZIK

Take 30 to 45 minutes for each interview. Have one person conduct the interview first. Then, switch roles and conduct the second interview. Listen with heart. Enjoy. Feel love. Be blessed.

Our wedding was many years ago. The celebration continues to this day.

—*Gene Perret*

1. Tell me the story of how you first knew you were in love. What were we doing? How did you know you were in love? What were your feelings and hopes? Which of those feelings and hopes have not only endured, but have grown and been strengthened over the years?

   A happy marriage is a long conversation which always seems too short.

   —*Andre Maurois*

2. Over the past 40 years, there have been many times when the moment has been perfect, and you've wanted to freeze that moment and come back to it again and again. Tell me about one of those moments. What were we doing? Who was there? What about the moment made it so perfect? What did we see, hear, touch, taste, and smell? Re-create that moment for me now.

   A single man has not nearly the value he would have in a state of union. He is an incomplete animal. He resembles the odd half of a pair of scissors.

   —*Benjamin Franklin*

3. What are the qualities that we both bring to this marriage that are complementary, like two matching halves of the scissors? What do you bring and what do I bring that match together perfectly to create an exceptional partnership?

4. A good pair of scissors has a set of sharp blades. What does each bring that cuts the other to the core—and in doing so, brings about growth, prompts forgiveness, and stretches the other?

Carol Anne Kozik, MS, CS, Learning Curve Associates, is pleased to share this enlivening interview guide to adapt to your couples experience.

A wedding anniversary is the celebration of love, trust, partnership, tolerance, and tenacity. The order varies for any given year.

—*Paul Sweeney*

5. What have the past five years asked us to celebrate? What have we learned, gained, and discovered in ourselves and in each other? How has that changed us?

    A successful marriage requires falling in love many times, always with the same person.

    —*Mignon McLaughlin,* The Second Neurotic's Notebook, *1966*

6. Looking into the next five years, what three wishes do we have for each other? What do we wish individually for each other and for us as a partnership?

After the two interviews, look at the following question together and share.

Chains do not hold a marriage together. It is threads, hundreds of tiny threads, which sew people together through the years.

—*Simon Signoret*

7. As we reflect on these stories and responses, what are the threads that have sewn us together? What stands out, or speaks to our hearts, as we listen to one another?

INTERVIEW WITH MY VALENTINE

Building the life we want together sits on a foundation of commitment, is stabilized through deliberate hard work, is uplifted by fun, and is held together by the bonds of love and spirit.

As you interview your valentine, listen for what touches you most, reminds you of why you are valentines, and offers you inspiration for your future together.

1. What are two or three of the most inspiring or rewarding experiences of our time together? Please tell me one of the stories.

2. What first attracted you to me (qualities, behaviors, potential, etc.)? What do you value most about me now?

3. How has our relationship helped or benefited you the most?

4. What challenges, disappointments, or roadblocks have we successfully addressed together?

5. What three things do you commit to do to increase the strength and vitality of our relationship?

APPRECIATIVE INQUIRY INTERVIEW PROTOCOL: LIFE-GIVING RELATIONSHIPS

JEN HETZEL SILBERT

1. Looking back at your past, tell me about a time when you felt most alive, most ful-filled, or most excited—a time when you can say you were living out a personal calling, something you've always wanted to do or dreamt of doing. What was it and what about it made it so spectacular? Share with me how this experience made you feel, what you valued most about it.

2. Now, looking at your entire experience with me—from the day we first met to now—tell me about a time when you felt most alive, most fulfilled, or most excited for us to be together. What was happening and what were we doing? Tell the story in detail:
   - What made it exciting?
   - Who/what else was involved?
   - What was it about me that helped make you feel so alive?

3. Let's talk about some things you value deeply—specifically, the things you value about yourself and your relationships with the people you love most.
   - Without being humble, what do you value most about yourself as a person?
   - What do you value about the relationships you share with special friends and family members?
   - What do you value about the relationship we've created together? What is the most important thing this relationship has contributed to your life?

4. What do you experience as the core factors that give life to this relationship? Give some examples of how you experience those factors.

5. What three wishes would you make to heighten the vitality and health of this rela-tionship?

6. Fast-forward to five years from now. Your wishes have come true, and life, as you know it, is better than you could ever have imagined. From our relationship to our lives at work, with friends, with family, and at home, we have a lot to be grateful for. What's happening? Tell me in detail the images you see.

7. What small steps/changes can you make today that will get you closer to making this future image a reality? Further, what support will you need from others in order to take those steps fearlessly?

GUIDELINES FOR COUPLES' COMMUNICATION

GET SPECIFIC

Use "videotalk." Describe what you are talking about so clearly that your partner could imagine seeing or hearing it on a videotape. If the person can't picture what you are saying or imagine hearing it, you aren't being specific enough to ensure your message will be heard. There is too much room for misinterpretation when you use vague words. Avoid giving your opinions, interpretations, or generalizations when you are having communication problems. They are invitations to misunderstandings and conflicts.

AVOID THE BLAME GAME OR DECIDING WHO IS REALLY RIGHT

Relationships are either win/win or lose/lose. If either of you loses, you both lose, because the relationship suffers. While it is tempting to get righteous or prove your partner wrong, it sets up a barrier to understanding and listening. Instead, imagine for a moment that there is another way of seeing the situation that might be different from how you see it.

BE ACCOUNTABLE FOR WHAT YOU SAY OR DO

Each of us has a choice about what we say and do, no matter how we feel. Don't excuse your behavior or blame it on others or on your childhood.

STICK WITH THE RECENT PAST WHEN YOU TALK ABOUT PROBLEMS

It is harder to change the past than the present and the future. People forget and disagree about what happened in the distant past.

ACKNOWLEDGE YOUR PARTNER'S FEELINGS AND POINTS OF VIEW

Listening to and acknowledging the other person's feelings and points of view can bypass many arguments and misunderstandings. Don't try to correct others or rebut their points of view or feelings. Just listen. See if you can understand what the other person is trying to communicate. You don't have to agree with what they are saying, but don't dismiss or minimize their feelings or tell them what is wrong with them for feeling that way.

NOTICE AND GIVE YOUR PARTNER AND YOUR RELATIONSHIP CREDIT FOR THE GOOD STUFF

It's all too easy to focus on the problems in relationships. Did your partner talk to you about something he or she would usually have avoided? Give the other person credit for that, even if you are upset about what they said. Did you two talk out something that you usually would have gotten stuck on? Mention it and acknowledge it to each other.

BREAK YOUR PATTERNS

It takes two to tango, so start doing the fox-trot and find out what happens. Change your part of any pattern that isn't working. Do anything that is not cruel, unethical, or distasteful to your partner that would be different from what you usually do in the situation. Remember: Insanity is doing the same thing over and over again and expecting different results. You can change your part of the pattern and invite your partner to change.

HOW TO SOLVE RELATIONSHIP PROBLEMS

IF IT AIN'T BROKE . . .

If things are going well in some area, you don't have to change that area or doubt yourself or the relationship. Determine what is working and do more of that.

STOP LISTENING TO EXPERTS

These days, you can find yourself doing something kind or compassionate for your partner and wonder if you are really being co-dependent. Or you may be reading a magazine article and suddenly decide that your relationship doesn't really make it, according to the article's guidelines. But remember: You are your own relationship expert. Trust your intuition and your common sense. Don't let outside experts (not just the ones in magazines or on television talk shows, but also your well-intentioned friends, coworkers, or relatives) talk you out of something you like or into something that you know isn't right for you.

DO SOMETHING DIFFERENT

They say that the only difference between a rut and a grave is the dimensions, and some couples have gotten into pretty deep ruts. Try changing anything you do in the relationship when you have problems (keep it ethical and safe, of course). If you usually argue in the bedroom, go into the kitchen and have the same discussion by writing it out on paper to one another and passing notes. If you usually fall asleep during the evening news, go bowling one night. Break out of your usual ruts by doing something completely out of character for you. If you continue to do what you usually do, you'll probably continue to get the usual responses and results.

FIND A DIFFERENT WAY TO LOOK AT THINGS

There's an old saying: Nothing is as dangerous as an idea when it is the only one you have. We are all prisoners of our limited points of view, and we have a tendency to think our point of view is the only correct way of seeing things, especially when we are upset. So, when you are stuck or unhappy, find another way of looking at it. Think of the situation from another angle. For example, how would you be thinking of this situation if it involved your child or your best friend instead of your spouse or partner?

CREATING OR RENEWING INTIMACY

Intimacy is personal for every relationship. Find out what helps each of you feel or sustain closeness and affection in your relationship. Here are some hints about some areas to examine and things to try to create, enhance, or sustain intimacy.

SPENDING TIME TOGETHER

Most people who feel close to one another spend a certain amount of time alone with each other. In busy times, with the demands of children and work, some couples find that they leave their time together as the last thing on their agenda. It might be important to put some special effort into scheduling or carving out some time regularly to spend with each other without distractions.

GET PHYSICAL

Most couples who report intimacy find that they touch each other in little ways when they are together: holding hands, sitting close, giving hugs when greeting or parting, touching the other person's elbow or shoulder when talking, and so on. In more private settings, there is more sexual touching. Has the touch or physical contact gone out of your relationship? Can you begin to reinstate it with simple gestures, like giving each other back rubs or holding hands while watching television? That might go a long way toward restoring or sustaining feelings of closeness.

BE VULNERABLE

Telling each other things that are risky to say, because you might be hurt or criticized by the other person, is a way to create or restore intimacy. Couples often share their hopes, dreams, and vulnerable feelings early on during courtship, but less so as time goes on. Many a midlife crisis is brought on by one partner feeling that he or she can no longer share deep, vulnerable feelings with his or her partner. Take a chance with your partner by sharing something a bit risky. It could open the door to intimacy.

DROP JUDGMENTS AND COMMUNICATE COMPASSION AND ADMIRATION

One of the barriers to intimacy is the feeling that your partner doesn't like or respect you or that you are being judged. Try dropping your critical feelings about your partner and developing some compassion or understanding or acceptance of quirks or nondestructive habits. Does he love baseball? Instead of belittling his passion, try supporting him in his interest. Does she cry at movies? Don't scoff and tell her she is being too sentimental, but give her the message that she is okay and you admire her for crying when she sees sad things.

POCKET EMERGENCY GUIDELINES

DO SOMETHING DIFFERENT

Don't keep doing the same thing. Change any pattern that is under your influence. Don't do anything dangerous or unethical, but get creative. Blow your partner's stereotype of you. Think about what you would normally do next and do something different.

GET SPECIFIC (USE ACTION TALK RATHER THAN BLAMING OR VAGUE WORDS)

Don't give theories or use general words. Describe the situation in a more objective way, stating what you can see or hear.

PRACTICE COMPASSIONATE LISTENING

Even if you feel attacked or don't understand your partner's actions or words, imagine that he or she is feeling scared or hurt at the moment when there are problems. Try getting into your partner's shoes or skin and imagining or trying to understand how he or she is seeing or feeling in this situation. Be sure that you understand and that your partner feels understood before you respond.

DON'T DO ANYTHING DRASTIC OR MAKE HASTY DECISIONS

In the heat of the moment, we might make decisions or take action out of anger, hurt, fear, or frustration. Take a few deep breaths and wait to calm down and get some distance before you make any hasty decisions or take impulsive actions. If necessary, take a timeout well before you say or do something you will later regret.

THINK!

While emotions provide important information when you are making decisions, doing what feels right at the moment will often cause problems.

USE THE PAST

Think about what has worked in similar situations in the past and consider how you can use that to help you this time.

PLAN AHEAD

Write down any notes that you think might help. You may want to include such things as phone numbers you can call or words you want to use in a tough situation.

GETTING OVER AN AFFAIR

People and relationships can and do heal from affairs. While each situation is unique, there are some general principles you may find helpful in moving on from such a painful and conflict-filled situation.

For the person who has had the affair:

Be accountable. Don't give excuses that claim you had no choice in the matter (like "She came on to me," "You were unfaithful years ago, so I was justified," or "We weren't having enough sex.").

Acknowledge what you did. You lied and your credibility is in doubt to your partner. Now is the time to step up and tell the truth. That doesn't mean to go into all the details, but rather to own up to your betrayal.

Take reasonable measures to rebuild trust (e.g., be where you say you're going to be and be there when you say you will). Be extra careful not to hide anything about what you are doing, however trivial it may seem to you or however much you are afraid it might hurt your partner. You don't have to share every passing feeling, but don't lie about your activities.

Apologize, and offer to make amends if possible. Acknowledge that what you did hurt your partner and offer your apologies. Ask your partner what you could do to make amends, if anything.

For the person who has been betrayed:

Don't badmouth your partner to your family or friends. They will, of course, side with you. It will come back to haunt you if you stay together, because your friends and family will be alienated from your partner or critical of you for getting back together with him or her. That doesn't mean you shouldn't seek support from your friends or family. Just be careful about how you talk about the situation.

Don't stalk or check up on your partner constantly. Either the person is going to be trustworthy or not. You'll eventually find out if you are being betrayed again. You can take reasonable precautions and do random checks to reassure yourself, but don't make it your waking preoccupation.

Don't ask detailed questions. Often you'll hear things that will haunt you for years, images that you will find hard to forget or get over. Once you know the broad outlines of what happened, let it rest for a while. If you find you are still haunted by those questions, try doing a ritual (discussed next) to help let it go. Or have your partner write out or record all the details and put the record of the affair in a safe-deposit box; give the key to a friend with instructions not to let you have the key for a year. If you still feel the need to know, go and look at the material after a year. Most people don't want to see it by then, as they have achieved some distance and don't want to open the whole painful mess again.

Do a ritual of letting go or moving on. This involves symbolically letting some emotion or situation go by physically getting rid of something that represents or symbolizes the unfinished business. For example, you might write a letter about everything you feel or want to say about the affair and then burn the pages you have written. Or you might get a picture of the person your partner had the affair with, tear it up, and throw the pieces into the ocean. One person got a key chain with the name of the person her husband had an affair with on it and drove back and forth over the key chain with her car to let go of many of her angry feelings toward that woman. Find something physical that represents the unfinished feelings or situation and do something symbolic of releasing it.

DEALING WITH A PARTNER OR SPOUSE WITH A CHEMICAL ABUSE PROBLEM

DON'T ARGUE ABOUT DIAGNOSES

One of the major hassles that couples get into regarding drug and alcohol problems is that one partner tries to convince the other that that person is really a drug addict or alcoholic. That is fine if your partner is open to accepting this label, but much of the time people aren't convinced their problem is that serious or merits that diagnosis. Contrary to what you may have read or heard, many people deal successfully with substance abuse problems without ever accepting the labels of addiction or alcoholism. The more important issue is to deal with the drinking or drug-taking behavior and its consequences. You can spend crucial time and energy on this more peripheral issue and alienate your partner in the process. Stick to what is important. Choose your battles wisely.

TALK IT OVER

Often the first step is to have a heart-to-heart talk with your partner about substance abuse and how you see it affecting your relationship and your family. State in no uncertain terms what you are asking your partner to do. Ask if there is anything you can do to help. After you have done this and have met any reasonable requests for assistance, accept that you have gone as far as you can to directly change your partner's abuse. If he or she doesn't make changes, you need to take steps designed more to take care of yourself than to change the behavior. Some people respond to consequences presented by the partner, but if you are providing consequences, don't do so with the intention of getting the user to change. It will usually be seen as manipulation.

SET CLEAR BOUNDARIES AND MAKE SPECIFIC AGREEMENTS REGARDING THE PROBLEMS RELATED TO THE SUBSTANCE USE

A better approach than arguing about labels is to set clear boundaries for what is acceptable and what is unacceptable or dangerous behavior and to stick to those boundaries. "Clear" means setting the boundaries in a specific way so that you and your partner both know when those boundaries are honored and when they are violated. For example, if your partner routinely tells you that he or she will be home at a certain time and shows up late, make sure that the boundary is clear. "If you are going to be any more than 15 minutes later than you said you'd be, please call telling me what time you expect to be home." Or, if your partner has been missing work due to drinking, focus the boundary on getting to work consistently and make the limits clear and unmistakable. "If you miss any more days of work, I think you are putting your job at risk and hurting our family finances. I would like you to do what you need to do to get to work every day for the next month." In many cases, if you focus on the drinking itself, you are likely to get into an unproductive argument. But in some situations, you might be able to make a clear agreement about the amount or frequency of drinking.

DON'T MAKE EXCUSES FOR YOUR PARTNER'S SUBSTANCE USE

From decades of experience with drug and alcohol problems, we have learned that one of the things that can inadvertently keep these problems going much longer than they otherwise would have lasted is if one partner develops a habit of making excuses for the other partner's drug or alcohol use or buffering that person from the consequences of the behavior. If they are hung over, don't call in to work for them saying that they are sick when in reality you can't wake them up. Don't let them off the hook for inappropriate behavior just because they have been using drugs or alcohol. For example, if the person gets violent when drunk, don't explain the violence away as a result of the alcohol. Hold the person accountable for the violence (and the alcohol use).

TAKE CARE OF YOURSELF

When you travel on an airplane, they make an announcement during the initial safety orientation. "If there is an emergency, oxygen masks will drop from the overhead compartment. If you are traveling with small children, put your oxygen mask on first, and then assist your children with putting theirs on." Why is this? Because if you pass out, your children will be very unlikely to be able to help you, but you can help them if they pass out first. In a similar way, it may be important for you to take care of yourself first in situations in which drugs and alcohol have come to affect you and your family. What is the oxygen mask for you? Do you need to have a separate checking or savings account in order to take care of yourself and your children? Do you need to go to Al-Anon meetings while you are dealing with your partner's problem? Do you need to make sure you exercise and take vitamins regularly? Don't get so focused on your partner's problem that you neglect to care for yourself.

TALK WITH THE KIDS

Children usually know exactly what is going on with their parents. There is a well-known saying referring to the presence of alcohol problems in a family that aren't acknowledged: There's an elephant in the living room that nobody talks about. If the problem becomes serious enough, it may be time to talk with the children and explain the situation. Beware of labels and psychological theories. Just explain in a straightforward manner the problem that you or your partner is having with substance abuse and the plan you have to tackle it. Answer any of the children's questions as honestly as possible (without revealing anything inappropriate for children to know and without blaming anyone).

PREVENTING OR DEALING WITH VIOLENCE IN A RELATIONSHIP

BREAKING THE SECRECY, SILENCE, AND SHAME

One of the things that supports violence in a relationship is keeping it secret. Some people who are battered or hit think that somehow there is something about them that brings on the violence or that it says something shameful about them. We are finding out that many more people, men and women, are subjected to violence in the home than we ever imagined. If you can, let someone know. This is not only for the person being hurt, but for the person who is doing the hurting. Violence can often be handled more effectively when you admit that it is happening and get help and support from others to change it.

MINIMIZING VIOLENCE

Another thing that can keep violence going is for either partner or both of you to dismiss it as trivial or to minimize it. It is a natural human tendency to play down the difficult or embarrassing things that happen. One way to counteract this tendency is to record the incident of violence on tape or through writing just after it occurs. It is still fresh in your mind and harder to play down. Later, when you have dismissed it or you remember it as not being so bad, you can check your sense of it with the record you have made.

BEING ACCOUNTABLE

We all have choices about our behavior, no matter what the circumstances. Often in situations of violence, the person who strikes out denies this responsibility by blaming the violence on the other person or on things beyond their control ("She kept at me, so I hit her" or "I have a temper, just like my mother, so I can't help hitting when I get angry"). An important step in stopping violence is for each partner to take responsibility for his or her behavior and not to offer excuses that claim they have no choice about what they do.

LOOK TO THE TIMES WHEN VIOLENCE WAS LIKELY BUT YOU AVOIDED IT AS A MODEL

Most couples with a history of violence also have a history of preventing violence. Examine times when one or both of you felt there was a likelihood of violence, but something one or both of you did prevented it. Did you walk away for a time? Did you stop talking and just sit in silence for a time? Did you calm yourself down in some way? Was someone else in the house or nearby? Find the elements that helped prevent the eruption of violence and use those as a model for how to prevent or avoid it in the future.

DEVELOP A PREVENTION PLAN

Even if you can't identify previous solutions, can you sit down together and plan for how to prevent violence in the future? Experiment with things that you think would be helpful. Talk over the potential pitfalls or failures of such a plan so that it is as realistic as possible. Write it down so you can consult it when it is needed. Make an agreement that you'll both stick to the plan when the time comes.

MAKE A LIST OF WARNING SIGNS

Most couples can give a list of signs that violence is coming. Is it when one person's voice grows loud? Is it when you get into an argument late at night? Is it when one person starts to call the other names? Is it right after taking a drink and then starting a discussion? Identify warning signs of violence and then put into practice the prevention plan or things that worked previously to avoid violence.

MAKE AN ESCAPE PLAN

Even the best of plans can go amiss. We know from research that many people stay in relationships in which there is ongoing violence. So, it's best to prepare an escape plan for the times when violence erupts. Prepare a list of options for escape. Hide an extra set of car and house keys somewhere where you can get to them if you have to run out of the house (under the back step or at a neighbor's house). Stash some money or a credit card. Pack a bag for you or for yourself and the kids. Have the phone number of the battered women's shelter or a hotel handy. Post a list of emergency numbers for the police, the shelter, the ambulance, your counselor, the Alcoholics Anonymous sponsor, and so on.

DON'T TRY TO SOLVE PROBLEMS WHEN UNDER THE INFLUENCE

Drugs and alcohol are often a component of violence in relationships. Even if some issue is pressing, put off discussion of it until both of you are sober. If there is never such a time, it is a sign that you need help.

SOLVING SEXUAL PROBLEMS

WHEN YOU'RE HOT, YOU'RE HOT AND WHEN YOU'RE NOT, YOU'RE NOT

Don't try to force yourself to feel sexual excitement when you are not feeling it. Sometimes when men lose their erections, they become self-conscious and try to force what had been a natural process of sexual excitement. This usually has the exact opposite effect. The same goes for women, lubrication, and sexual excitement. Sometimes the lack of sexual excitement may be just temporary or due to the situation. In that case, just accepting this lack of excitement can help you get through this time. The next time, things will probably work just fine. Or the lack of sexual excitement may be due to more long-term factors, such as a medical condition or medications that interfere with arousal or response. Or it may be an indication of boredom or problems in your sexual relationship or your relationship in general. Regardless of the reason for the lack of arousal, the suggestion remains the same. Don't try to force yourself to become aroused.

LET YOUR PARTNER KNOW WHAT FEELS GOOD (AND WHAT DOESN'T)

Think of sex as a bit like back-scratching. Your partner could have no way of knowing what feels good to you at the moment unless you let him or her know. This is sometimes hard for people to do in the realm of sex because they are not used to speaking openly about sexual matters, but it is crucial to break that silence and speak up if you want to enhance your sexual relationship.

GET CREATIVE

Get out of ruts. Try new positions, locations, talk, clothes, toys, and so on. Read each other fantasies you have found in books or magazines or written out of your imagination.

ASK FOR WHAT YOU WANT, BUT DON'T DEMAND IT

People don't usually respond well in sexual situations when they are feeling uncomfortable or forced to participate in something they don't like. So, make sure you are not coercing or forcing your partner to do things he or she doesn't want to do. At the same time, sometimes people don't speak up about what they desire or would like to try because they are afraid their partner wouldn't like it or would disapprove. You can at least bring the subject up to your partner and let him or her know there is no demand, but an interest in trying some sexual behavior.

SCHEDULE TIME

Don't always leave sex until late at night or assume it will happen spontaneously. You may have to schedule time out of your busy work, social, or family life for sexual encounters. Again, the key here is to take the pressure off. You are scheduling time to allow sexual interactions, but if the timing or the situation isn't right, just use that time to reconnect in any way you can. You might just give each other back rubs, or talk, or snuggle. If sex happens, great! If not, relax and enjoy this special time together.

FANTASIES AND DESIRES DON'T NECESSARILY EQUAL IDENTITY OR LEAD TO BEHAVIOR

Just because you fantasize about things, it doesn't necessarily indicate that you want to act those things out or have them happen in the real world. You may fantasize about being raped or having sex with someone of the same gender, but you may never want to experience that in reality.

This can also hold true for your sexual identity. Many people have attractions to people of the same sex, but don't define themselves as homosexual. Likewise, sometimes people who are homosexual have attractions to people of the opposite sex, but still think of themselves as gay or lesbian. Your sexual identity is partly a matter of where you feel comfortable and what your attractions are, but it is mainly a function of how you choose to define yourself. You may not have much choice about what or who turns you on, but your identity is much more a matter of choice and preference. Some people live their whole lives being primarily attracted to one sex, yet define themselves in a very different way. Call it denial or whatever you will, but sexual identity is a political act and each person must sort out his or her own politics.

You *can* let yourself feel, fantasize, or think anything you experience sexually. Your experience does not have to determine your choices in life or define you.

MEDICATIONS, ALCOHOL/DRUGS, AND MEDICAL CONDITIONS CAN AFFECT SEXUAL DESIRE AND RESPONSES

In small amounts, drugs or alcohol may help you relax inhibitions, but in larger amounts they can interfere with sexual functioning. Medications can also interfere with sexual desire or functioning. If you are using medications and experiencing problems of desire or functioning, check with a physician or pharmacist who is knowledgeable in such matters and make adjustments in your prescription if necessary. If you are regularly using significant amounts of drugs or alcohol, try decreasing and then stopping your substance use and find out if your desire or response returns. If it doesn't, there may be a medical condition that is affecting your desire. Again, check with a physician about these matters.

IN SEARCH OF THE BIG O

Don't get so hung up on the goal that you ignore or rush the process. Trying too hard to have an orgasm can prevent you from having one or enjoying it when it arrives. On the other hand, if you never or rarely have orgasms, you can make adjustments so that this becomes a more regular part of your sexual experience. Use the other suggestions here to enhance the likelihood of experiencing orgasms.

What about premature ejaculation? Slow down, stop moving, and pay attention to when an orgasm is approaching. Many men feel they have to perform or keep moving to give their partners pleasure. Delaying ejaculation is a skill that can be learned. Work together to help him learn to slow down and enjoy the process.

What about having simultaneous orgasms? It is possible, again with good communication and with taking the pressure off. Some couples have this experience quite regularly, whereas others have such different timing that it is unlikely they will coordinate orgasms.

TRAIN YOUR THERAPIST

TELL YOUR THERAPIST WHAT WORKS AND HAS WORKED FOR YOU

Each person and couple is unique. You can help your therapist by indicating which styles and questions he or she uses work best for you as an individual and as a couple. That does not mean that you run the therapy. The therapist does have some expertise and good reasons for doing what he or she is doing, but a good therapist also has some room for flexibility. If you have been in counseling before and found some aspect or method particularly helpful, let your therapist know about that.

LET YOUR THERAPIST KNOW WHEN HE OR SHE DOES SOMETHING RIGHT

Therapy can be a difficult and challenging field of work. Your therapist sees people when they are at their most stressed and sometimes their most impatient. Sometimes the therapist doesn't know whether he or she has been helpful, because people don't return or because change takes some time. So, most therapists appreciate hearing that they have done something that worked or was helpful. This can also make your therapy experience more productive, since your therapist will have your feedback to guide him or her in future attempts to help you.

TELL YOUR THERAPIST YOUR EXPECTATIONS

If you attend therapy expecting to go back to your childhood to find the roots of the problem and your therapist focuses on the present, you are bound to be frustrated if that expectation isn't brought up and discussed before you proceed. Also, you might indicate how long you had anticipated you would attend therapy, and how often, to make sure you and the therapist are on the same track.

TELL YOUR THERAPIST WHAT DOESN'T WORK

Like telling your therapist your expectations and letting him or her know what has worked or is helping, letting your therapist know when something *isn't* helping is important. This includes what is happening at home as well as during your therapy sessions. This gives the opportunity for midcourse corrections in the therapy process.

TELL YOUR THERAPIST YOUR OBJECTIONS

Some people think that they shouldn't speak up about their worries or objections to their therapist's suggestions, but a free and frank discussion about any misgiving helps your therapist deal with your concerns and make any adjustments to ensure a higher likelihood of success.

ASK QUESTIONS

Ask about the therapy process, fees, any suggestions or methods, the therapist's training and qualifications, or anything else you are curious about. If the subject gets too personal or the therapist considers the questions intrusive or inappropriate, he or she will let you know.

DEMAND THAT YOUR THERAPIST SPEAK IN EVERYDAY LANGUAGE

All professions have jargon and buzzwords. If your therapist suggests "an MMPI to check out whether you have MPD or ADHD," you have a perfect right to have a translation in language you understand.

RELATIONSHIP RESCUE: TEN METHODS FOR RESOLVING RELATIONSHIP CRISES

This material is designed to help you quickly break through relationship impasses and resolve crises. Use any of these methods that make sense to you and that work.

CHANGE YOUR USUAL CONFLICT PATTERNS OR STYLE

If your voice usually gets loud, soften your voice volume. If you usually run away or withdraw during an argument, stay put. If you usually try to argue your point of view with a lawyer's precision and aggressiveness, just state your feelings in the matter and let it rest. If you usually interrupt other people's talking to rebut or refute what they are saying, just listen until they are done talking, then repeat what they have said back to them and ask whether you have understood what their point is or what their feelings are. If you usually point your finger during an argument, sit on your hands instead.

Or you might try changing the mode of expression you usually use to communicate. If you are talking, switch to a piece of paper and write out what you have to say. Or record it into a tape recorder and ask your partner to listen to it in another room.

Another way to change your usual conflict patterns or style is to change the location or the timing. Instead of arguing in the living room, go to the front seat of the car or to a restaurant to argue. If you usually argue late at night, make an appointment for the next afternoon and have the argument then. Or limit the argument to 10 minutes using the kitchen timer and then take a break for 10 minutes, getting some physical distance from each other and remaining silent. Then argue another 10 minutes, followed by another 10 minutes of silence. Continue this pattern until the issue is resolved or you both agree to stop.

DO A 180: CHANGE YOUR USUAL PURSUER-DISTANCER PATTERN

This is a variation on the preceding method, but it is more specific. Most couples fall into a typical pattern of who pursues and who withdraws, both in the relationship and during conflicts. Figure out which part of the pattern you usually play out and change your style (from the person who withdraws to the person who stays or pursues or vice versa). Both of you or either one of you can make these changes.

CATCH YOUR PARTNER DOING SOMETHING RIGHT

Make note of and speak to your partner about everything that you can think of to give him or her credit for in the recent past. Tell your partner about times when you felt cared about, helped, or understood by him or her and the specific things that led you to feel that way. Mention things that your partner did that you admired or were pleasantly surprised about. Catch the other person doing or almost doing something differently that you want him or her to do and offer praise for it. Notice when the other person does something during an argument that seems fairer, more compassionate, or friendlier than usual or that helps you to resolve things. (Hint: You can also catch yourself doing something right and silently give yourself credit. Note that righteousness is not encouraged. Rather, notice when you are being flexible, compassionate, and understanding.)

UNPACK VAGUE, BLAMING, AND LOADED WORDS INTO VIDEOTALK (ACTION DESCRIPTIONS)

Notice what words you are using that get a rise out of your partner and find a way to use less loaded or provocative words or phrases. For example, you might find that when you say things like "You're being selfish" or "You're just like your father," your partner reacts badly. The simplest way to defuse such phrases and words is to translate them into action descriptions or what could be called "videotalk." Videotalk refers to using words that describe what you could see and hear on a videotape, rather than using more vague or judgmental words. So, instead of saying, "Well, when you were judging me, I got defensive," you could try saying, "When you pointed your finger at me and said I was immature, I got defensive."

CHANGE YOUR COMPLAINTS INTO ACTION REQUESTS

Probably the most crucial area in which to use videotalk is in telling your partner what is bothering you about the relationship or what he or she is doing with or around you. Instead of indicting the person for personality flaws or having the wrong feelings, describing the behavior in videotalk usually seems less blaming and is more likely to give a hint about what the person might change to make things better.

MAKE A SPECIFIC CHANGE PLAN

Often we do better in making changes if we sit and plan a strategy of action, write it down, and check back on what we have written down on a regular basis. This can be done with or without your partner. In making such a plan, it is important to include specific actions that you or your partner or both of you are going to take, a timeline for taking such actions or a commitment to how frequently you will take such actions, and a plan for how and when to check back on the plan to see if it's working or to make adjustments.

FOCUS ON HOW YOU (NOT YOUR PARTNER) CAN CHANGE, AND TAKE RESPONSIBILITY FOR MAKING THAT CHANGE

Even if your partner is the source of the problem, this method involves you assuming responsibility for making changes. This is based on the idea that people are responsive to changes around them. If you stop doing the tango and start doing the fox-trot, your partner will have a harder time doing the old tango steps. So, figure out places in the usual course of things that go wrong and in which you have a moment of choice to do something different and new that isn't harmful or destructive.

BLOW YOUR PARTNER'S STEREOTYPE OF YOU

Sometimes the people we live with get a stereotyped impression of who we are, and we confirm that by always playing our typical roles. Figure out what your partner's stereotype of you is (you never do any work around the house, or you are always critical when he wants to watch football) and make a determined effort to shatter those expectations. Surprise yourself and your partner by doing something that would be entirely out of character for you (but again, make sure it is not destructive or mean-spirited).

COMPASSIONATE LISTENING

Sometimes the simplest solution is just to stop and listen to what your partner is saying and imagine how he or she could be feeling that way or seeing things in that light. Don't try to defend yourself, correct others' perceptions, or talk them out of their feelings. Just put yourself in their position. Try to hear how they understand, interpret, and feel about the situation, and imagine how you would feel or act if you were seeing things that way. Express that understanding to them and let them know how difficult it must be for them, given how they are feeling about the situation.

When you are stuck in a relationship problem, things can seem hopeless. This handout has given you some ideas and methods you can use to get yourself unstuck. If problems persist or you find yourself too discouraged to even consider these methods, it is wise to seek the help of a marriage or relationship counselor.

DEALING WITH THE DEATH OF A CHILD

It is said that the worst thing that can befall parents is the death of their child. This certainly seems to be reflected in the alarmingly high divorce rate among parents who have lost a child. Divorce is not inevitable, though, and many marriages do make it through this terrible and challenging experience. One of the major challenges seems to be coming to terms with differences in grieving styles. One partner may wish to stop talking about the child's death and the other may want to talk a great deal about it to process the grief, thus creating further stress at an already stressful time.

Acknowledge that each person has his or her style and timing. Some people like to hold on to the child and some prefer to let go. Some prefer to speak about their grief or cry about it, whereas others feel numb or want to process it in silence. There is no right way or wrong way to deal with death.

The same is true with books and pamphlets about the grieving process. Nobody can tell anyone else the right way to grieve, the right timing for grieving, or the proper stages for grief. Even if you don't think you are doing it correctly, or you are numb, or are overly upset, feel relief, or feel guilt, these can all be part of a normal grief process. Don't let anyone tell you what is right for you if it doesn't fit for you.

Some people find that making a donation, doing public speaking, or working to raise public awareness or make some changes in the world can be ways to give the child's death some meaning and find some higher purpose to cope with the loss. What would give your child's death some meaning? What contribution could his or her death, as terrible as it is, make to others?

Some find that instead of letting the child go, they can imagine that the child is there to give them advice and consolation at this time of grief (and perhaps for years into the future). Friends and family, even professionals, will often urge you to say good-bye. Perhaps it would be best for you to say hello again. What would your child say to you now to help you cope with the situation?

GENERIC ASSIGNMENT FORM

ACTION PLANS/IDEAS TO CONSIDER

Your Name: _____   Your Address: _____

Phone Number: _____   City, State, Zip: _____

Next Appointment Time/Date: _____   Today's Date: _____

REFERENCES

Hudson, P., & O'Hanlon, W. (1991). *Rewriting love stories: Brief marital therapy*. New York: Norton.

O'Hanlon, B., & Hudson, P. (1995). *Love is a verb: How to stop analyzing your relationship and start making it great!* New York: Norton.

O'Hanlon, S., & O'Hanlon, B. (1998). Love is a noun (Except when it's a verb): A solution-oriented approach to intimacy. In L. Sperry & J. Carlson (Eds.), *The intimate couple*. Washington, DC: Brunner/Mazel.

ABOUT THE CD-ROM

INTRODUCTION

This appendix provides you with the information on the contents of the CD that accompanies this book. For the latest and greatest information, please refer to the ReadMe file located at the root of the CD.

SYSTEM REQUIREMENTS

- A computer with a processor running at 120 Mhz or faster
- At least 32 MB of total RAM installed on your computer; for best performance, we recommend at least 64MB
- A CD-ROM drive

Note: Many popular word processing programs are capable of reading Microsoft Word files. However, users should be aware that a slight amount of formatting might be lost when using a program other than Microsoft Word.

USING THE CD WITH WINDOWS

To install the items from the CD to your hard drive, follow these steps:

1. Insert the CD into your computer's CD-ROM drive.
2. The CD-ROM interface will appear. The interface provides a simple point-and-click way to explore the contents of the CD.

If the opening screen of the CD-ROM does not appear automatically, follow these steps to access the CD:

1. Click the Start button on the left of the taskbar and then choose Run from the menu that pops up. (In Windows Vista and Windows 7, skip this step.)
2. In the dialog box that appears, type d:\setup.exe. (If your CD drive is not drive d, use the appropriate letter in place of d.) This brings up the CD interface described in the preceding set of steps. (In Windows Vista or Windows 7, type d:\setup.exe in the Start > Search text box.)

USING THE CD WITH A MAC

1. Insert the CD into your computer's CD-ROM drive.
2. When the CD-ROM icon appears on your desktop, double-click the icon.
3. Double-click the Start icon.
4. The CD-ROM interface will appear. The interface provides a simple point-and-click way to explore the contents of the CD.

WHAT'S ON THE CD

The following sections provide a summary of the software and other materials you'll find on the CD.

Content

Includes all 70 homework assignments from the book in Word format. Homework assignments can be customized, printed out, and distributed to clients in an effort to extend the therapeutic process outside the office. All documentation is included in the folder named "Content."

Applications

The following applications are on the CD:

OpenOffice.org

OpenOffice.org is a free multi-platform office productivity suite. It is similar to Microsoft Office or Lotus SmartSuite, but OpenOffice.org is absolutely free. It includes word processing, spreadsheet, presentation, and drawing applications that enable you to create professional documents, newsletters, reports, and presentations. It supports most file formats of other office software. You should be able to edit and view any files created with other office solutions. Certain features of Microsoft Word documents may not display as expected from within OpenOffice.org. For system requirements, go to www.openoffice.org.

Software can be of the following types:

- Shareware programs are fully functional, free, trial versions of copyrighted programs. If you like particular programs, register with their authors for a nominal fee and receive licenses, enhanced versions, and technical support.
- Freeware programs are free, copyrighted games, applications, and utilities. You can copy them to as many computers as you like—for free—but they offer no technical support.
- GNU software is governed by its own license, which is included inside the folder of the GNU software. There are no restrictions on distribution of GNU software. See the GNU license at the root of the CD for more details.

- Trial, demo, or evaluation versions of software are usually limited either by time or functionality (such as not letting you save a project after you create it).

Troubleshooting

If you have difficulty installing or using any of the materials on the companion CD, try the following solutions:

- **Turn off any antivirus software that you may have running.** Installers sometimes mimic virus activity and can make your computer incorrectly believe that a virus is infecting it. (Be sure to turn the antivirus software back on later.)

- **Close all running programs.** The more programs that you're running, the less memory is available to other programs. Installers also typically update files and programs; if you keep other programs running, installation may not work properly.

- **Reference the README file.** Please refer to the README file located at the root of the CD for the latest product information at the time of publication.

USER ASSISTANCE

If you have trouble with the CD-ROM, please call the Wiley Product Technical Support phone number at (800) 762-2974. Outside the United States, call 1 (317) 572-3994. You can also contact Wiley Product Technical Support at http://support.wiley.com. John Wiley & Sons will provide technical support only for installation and other general quality control items. For technical support of the applications themselves, consult the program vendor or author.

To place additional orders or to request information about other Wiley products, please call (800) 225-5945.